Skills & Values: Lawyering Process

Carolina Academic Press
Skills & Values Series
David I. C. Thomson, Series Editor

Skills & Values: Administrative Law
Alfred C. Aman, Jr.

Skills & Values: Alternative Dispute Resolution: Negotiation, Mediation, Collaborative Law and Arbitration
John Burwell Garvey and Charles B. Craver

Skills & Values: Civil Procedure, Second Edition
Catherine Ross Dunham and Don C. Peters

Skills & Values: Constitutional Law
William D. Araiza, Thomas E. Baker, Olympia Duhart, and Steven I. Friedland

Skills & Values: Contracts, Second Edition
William J. Woodward, Jr. and Candace M. Zierdt

Skills & Values: Criminal Law
Andrew Taslitz, Lenese Herbert, and Eda Katharine Tinto

Skills & Values: Criminal Procedure
Susan L. Kay and William Cohen

Skills & Values: Discovery Practice, Third Edition
David I. C. Thomson

Skills & Values: Evidence, Second Edition
John B. Mitchell and Rick T. Barron

Skills & Values: Family Law
Justine A. Dunlap

Skills & Values: Federal Income Taxation
Michelle L. Drumbl and Deborah S. Kearns

Skills & Values: Intellectual Property
Courtney G. Lytle

Skills & Values: Lawyering Process: Legal Writing and Advocacy, Second Edition
David I. C. Thomson

Skills & Values: Legal Negotiating, Third Edition
Charles B. Craver

Skills & Values: Property Law
Brian D. Shannon and Gerry W. Beyer

Skills & Values: The First Amendment, Second Edition
Charles W. Rhodes and Paul E. McGreal

Skills & Values: Torts
Christine Ver Ploeg and Peter B. Knapp

Skills & Values: Trusts and Estates
Roger W. Andersen and Karen Boxx

Skills & Values: Lawyering Process

Legal Writing and Advocacy

SECOND EDITION

David I. C. Thomson
Professor of Practice and
John C. Dwan Professor for Online Learning
University of Denver, Sturm College of Law

Carolina Academic Press
Durham, North Carolina

ISBN 978-1-5310-0815-4
eISBN 978-1-5310-0816-1
LCCN 2017950953

Carolina Academic Press
700 Kent Street
Durham, North Carolina 27701
Telephone (919) 489-7486
Fax (919) 493-5668
www.cap-press.com

Printed in the United States of America

To Kathy
With gratitude for
all your love and support

Contents

Introduction xv
How this Book Is Organized xvii

Acknowledgments xix

Chapter 1 · The Lawyering Process 3
Introduction 3
What Lawyers Do 4
Legal Research 5
Reading Legal Materials 6
Organizing What You Find 6
Basic Legal Documents 6
Legal Writing Style 7
Citation 8
Advocacy 8
Conclusion 9
Further Reading 9
Exercise 10

Chapter 2 · Legal Work 11
Introduction 11
Law Offices 12
The Importance of Self-Care 12
Further Reading 13
Exercise 14

Chapter 3 · The Legal System 15
Introduction 15
How the American Legal System Is Designed 15
Further Reading 18
Exercise 19

Chapter 4 · Reading the Law 21
Introduction 21
Reading Statutes 21
Reading Cases 22
Case Briefing 24
Synthesizing Several Cases 24

Further Reading 25
Exercise 26

Chapter 5 · Legal Research 27
Introduction 27
Developing a Research Strategy 27
Types of Legal Research 28
Sources of Law and Legal Information 29
Primary Sources 29
Secondary Sources 30
Finding Aids/Updating Sources 30
Explanatory Sources 31
Legislative History 32
Interpreting and Using the Authority You Have Found 32
Controlling vs. Persuasive Authority 32
Good or Bad Case Law 32
Unpublished Opinions 33
Contrary Opinions 33
Tracking Your Research 33
When to Stop Researching 33
Further Reading 35
Exercise 36

Chapter 6 · Legal Memos 37
Introduction 37
The IRAC Format 38
Synthesis 38
Basic Format of a Legal Research Memo 39
Question Presented 39
Brief Answer 39
Statement of Facts 40
Discussion Section 40
The Conclusion 42
Email Memos 42
Oral Report 42
Further Reading 43
Exercises 44

Chapter 7 · Legal Citation 45
Introduction 45
What Is the Bluebook? 45
Why We Cite 45
When to Cite 46
Using the Bluebook 46
Key Elements of the Bluebook 46

The Index 47
The Tables 47
Cross-References 48
Tabbing the Bluebook 48
Formula for a Basic Case Citation 49
Formula for a Statute Citation 51
Id.: The Ultimate Short Form Citation 53
String Citations: How to Cite to More Than One Authority 54
Constructing a Journal or Law Review Citation 54
Formula for Creating a Citation to the Internet 55
Introductory Signals, B1.2 and R1.2 55
Parenthetical Information, Rule 1.5 56
Citing to Court Documents, B.17 57
The Name of the Document 57
Pinpoint Citations 57
Date 57
Examples of Record Citations 57
Citing to Quotations, Rule 5 57
Practice Exercise 1: When to Cite 59
Practice Exercise 2: Using the Index 59
Practice Exercise Answers 60
Further Reading 60
Exercise 61

Chapter 8 · Writing Well 63
Introduction 63
Knowing Your Audience 63
Clarity and Conciseness 63
Punctuation and Grammar 65
Writing Preparation 67
The Thick Outline 67
MindMapping 69
Further Reading 69
Exercise 70

Chapter 9 · Editing and Proofreading 71
Introduction 71
Editing 72
Proofreading 72
Further Reading 73
Exercise 74

Chapter 10 · Contract Drafting 75
Introduction 75
Purpose of a Contract 75

Language of Drafting 75
Structure of a Contract 76
Heading 76
Caption 77
Recitals 77
Definitions 77
Operative Language 78
Closing 79
Contract Disputes 79
1. Describing Characteristics or Categories 80
2. Modifiers 80
3. Synonyms 81
Further Reading 81
Exercise 82

Chapter 11 · Legal Persuasion 83
Introduction 83
Aristotle's Modes of Persuasion 83
Storytelling Your Theme 84
Literary Devices 85
Further Reading 86
Exercise 87

Chapter 12 · Legal Letters 89
Introduction 89
The Opinion Letter 89
The Demand Letter 90
The Settlement Letter 91
Professional Email 91
Further Reading 92
Exercise 93

Chapter 13 · Legal Briefs 95
Introduction 95
Ethics 95
Types of Arguments 95
Choosing Your Issues 96
Sections in the Brief 97
Introduction: Title Page, Table of Contents, Table of Authorities 97
Statement of the Issues 97
Statement of Facts 98
Statement of the Case 99
Summary of the Argument 99
The Argument 99
Responding to Opposing Arguments 100

Conclusion 101
Further Reading 101
Exercise 102

Chapter 14 · Oral Argument 103
Introduction 103
Trial Court — Motions Arguments 103
Appellate Court Arguments 104
Questions During Oral Arguments 106
Preparation for Oral Arguments 107
Further Reading 109
Exercise 110

Introduction

The first time I taught a legal writing and oral advocacy course was nearly 30 years ago. The students in that class have long since graduated and by now practiced law for many years. I am sure they have overcome the errors that I no doubt made in my first year of teaching. My recollection is that the director of the program gave me the class list but little else in terms of direction about what to do. In those days, there was nothing like the now quite mature pedagogy of teaching the course, worked out over the years since by my many colleagues in the field. Back then there was little to go on. I remember meeting with the class every Monday morning at 8:00 a.m., before putting in a full week of work as an associate in a New York City law firm. My Sundays were spent reviewing papers, providing feedback, and preparing for class.

I do not remember whether I assigned a textbook. If I did it might have been *Legal Method: Cases and Text Materials* (West, 1980) by Professors Jones, Kernochan, and Murphy at the Columbia Law School. As the title suggests, it was essentially a casebook that covered the legislative process and statutory interpretation. But it included very little about legal writing. Or it might have been *Introduction to Advocacy* (Foundation Press, 1981) which was produced by the Board of Student Advisors at Harvard Law. Aside from these works, I did not have much to choose from. In those days, there were no legal writing textbooks, at least not as we currently conceive them.

Today we have a plethora of such textbooks from longtime leaders in the field, scholars such as Helene Shapo, Linda Edwards, Charles Calleros, Anne Enquist, Richard Neumann, and Laurel Oates. Many of these books are now in their fifth or sixth edition. Teachers of the legal writing and advocacy course have a diverse and mature group of books to choose from when they decide on a text for their courses.

These works are large and comprehensive, covering every aspect of the subject. In contrast, this book aims to be shorter, more focused, and (I hope) more pedagogically flexible. First, it is a hybrid text, which means that only a portion of the text is printed, with the rest residing online. When a professor adopts this text, it comes with a fully populated website with supporting materials for the students in the course. Information about this online site can be obtained through Carolina Academic Press (CAP), and your school's publishing representative for CAP. On the companion site for the book, you will see a full Teacher's Manual as well (only available to the professor), with a suggested Fall and Spring semester Syllabus, rubrics, assignments that tie into the design of the book, and various supplemental materials. Also included is a suggested full problem set for the "closed memo" that most courses begin with. On the student portion of the site, there are numerous examples and supporting documents, each of which ties into each chapter in the print book.

As a result of the close integration between the print book and the online site, it would be unfair (or at least incomplete) to judge the print book alone, without reviewing the online site as well. All told, there is probably twice as much material online as what you hold in your hands. And, as noted, it is all customizable by the professor and immediately useable by the student as needed.

So, the first difference between this text and other such books is that this one is a hybrid text, which allows the book to be somewhat cheaper, and also allows for more interactive features in the online portion of the text than can be achieved in print. Second, it is based on the belief that students today need to read less and do more, to be active rather than passive. Aristotle said, "What we have to learn to do, we learn by doing." It is no secret to educators that our students are changing. Some assume this is a bad thing and lament the "short attention span" of the Google generation. But most teachers would rather, as teachers have for millennia, reach their students wherever they are with what they need. This book attempts to do that for a new generation of legal writing students.

Third, students are learning this material for the first time and perhaps do not need to read in the first year huge amounts of information about the writing process. Students certainly do need a deeper understanding later in law school, and in practice. But as they are first learning how to do, they need to do, rather than spend so much time reading about it. So the topics addressed in this book are covered (in the print text) at less depth than in the traditional legal writing textbooks. The chapters are designed to introduce the basic concepts of the fundamental lawyering skills—and to be supplemented with additional interactive information online. Lawyering and advocacy skills are learned through an iterative process of doing and failing, doing and failing, with the instructor providing support and feedback until success is achieved.

Finally, this book is designed for flexible use. Each professor has his or her own ways of teaching the course. The older textbooks all have their own approaches, which may not be fully in sync with how the professor treats the material. So the professor compensates by creating his or her own assignments, handouts, and examples. When the two differ, this can be confusing for students. A central idea behind this textbook is—as much as possible—to enable professors to assign limited amounts of reading and then use the online materials (and their own materials) in ways that best suit their individual approaches to the course.

The Carnegie Report (2007) criticized law school for, among other failings, not being intentional about the formation of professional identity among its students. Many law professors received this criticism quizzically since a course in professional responsibility has always been a part of legal education and indeed is required by the ABA. The report was responsible in part for this confusion because it unintentionally blurred the distinction between (1) the required course in professional responsibility and (2) a new concept introduced in the report—the formation of professional identity. But there is an important difference between these two concepts.

Professionalism includes, of course, such responsibilities as thoroughness, respect for opposing counsel and judges, and responding to clients in a timely fashion. *Professional identity* includes a lawyer's decisions about these behaviors, his or her sense of duty as an officer of the court and, perhaps most importantly, his or her sense of responsibility as part of a system that is engaged in upholding the rule of law. Teaching professional identity means we ask students to finish this sentence: "I am a lawyer and that means for me that I will resolve this ethical dilemma as follows ..." The Carnegie report is probably correct when it says that law schools do not do that very successfully.

The problem is that the formation of an identity is not something professors can "teach" per se. You cannot teach a person to form his or her own identity. Rather, professors need to create "situations" in which students can be confronted with ethical questions and reflect on the decisions they make, and be guided by us as teachers as they form their own professional identities. The Skills & Values series of textbooks offer materials to help teachers create these learning situations.

This book, as with the entire Skills & Values Series, is a new and different way to think of a legal text than any we have had in the past. It is designed to be adaptable and to help us teach students what they need to know to become well-rounded and skilled professionals. And it tries to tap into the ways our students learn best, so that we may successfully prepare them "*for their future, not our past.*"*

How this Book Is Organized

What follows are 14 chapters that provide students with an introduction to the key aspects of the Lawyering Process from understanding what lawyers do, to research, writing, citation, writing style, drafting, persuasion, and oral arguments. These chapters provide introductory reading on each topic, with supplemental reading sometimes offered by the professor, and examples, quizzes, checklists, and links provided online. After reading the assigned chapter for class, the student should next go to the online site to see what additional materials have been provided to read or work with before class. If the student would like more reading on a chapter topic, each of the chapters concludes with a short list of recommended further reading on that topic.

At the end of each chapter, the student will find an assignment or exercise. The professor may assign these, or may substitute his or her own assignment. There will also be opportunities for the student to identify and consider ethical questions that confront lawyers every day. They are designed to help the student along the journey to forming his or her own professional identity as a lawyer.

* David I. C. Thomson, *Law School 2.0: Legal Education for a Digital Age*, xi (2009).

There is also this thing called Google, but you have probably heard of it. Google search results are not always authoritative, but the Internet can be a tremendous guide to learning. The approach of this book is to encourage the student to customize his or her reading and learning on each of the topics and not feel limited to what is contained in the book. We all learn differently and each student should seek to take charge of his or her own legal education. Good lawyers are life-long learners, and it is not too early to cultivate that approach to everything about the law.

When students start law school, the journey seems long, and the path at times seems foggy and unclear. It is unsettling to join a discourse community where one does not even know what one does not know. But the good news is that the fog will gradually clear during the first year, and this course can be a port in the storm. It is the place where students can safely ask questions that might seem basic and naive, and where they can begin to make the connections between what they are learning in this course with what they are learning in their other courses. Before long, students in this course realize that they have learned a lot about how the legal system works, and their future role in it as lawyers, and the fog begins to clear.

David Thomson
University of Denver
May 14, 2017

Acknowledgments

As with any such effort, there are many others whose support and contributions went into this book, and I want to offer my thanks to them. I am grateful first to Cardozo Law School in New York City, for its willingness years ago to take a chance by hiring as an adjunct someone barely out of law school himself. I had, as I recall, 32 students in that first class, and while it was a lot of work on top of my practice, I remember my students as being engaged, hard working, and supportive. I was hooked on teaching and have remained so ever since. I owe a large debt of gratitude as well to the hundreds of students I have had since then in my Lawyering Process classes at the Sturm College of Law at the University of Denver, where I have taught for many years, the last 15 as a member of the full-time faculty. I hope, of course, these students would say they learned a lot from me, but it is truly I who learned a great deal from them. In many ways this book is the product of what they have taught me about how they learn this material, and what works best as they develop their skills in the course.

I have also over the years been supported and aided by an impressive array of teaching assistants and research assistants, many of whom have contributed directly to this book in one way or another. I have learned a lot from all of my TAs and RAs, especially in their thoughtful guidance about the learning styles of the current generation of students. They have given me feedback about many aspects of the course, particularly the reading materials I have assigned over the years. Among those TAs and RAs, I specifically thank: Chad Grell, Eileen Joy, Ian London, Kendra Beckwith, Megan Embrey, Kate Bartell Nowak, Jill Sage, Kelley Haun, Colton Johnston, Liz Deline, and Lisel Thompson. Also, I am grateful to former students Krista Nash and Logan Cornett, though not serving as TAs or RAs for me, gave me excellent feedback on early drafts of the book. I am indebted to all of these students for helping me to conceive the book and keep it oriented toward what students need when encountering the course material.

Naturally, I have learned a great deal from my colleagues in the LP Program at the University of Denver. They have been full of good ideas, which we have shared in a seamless process of collaboration and improvement. I am grateful to them for their ideas, support, and the collaborative spirit that we enjoy. In addition, I appreciate my colleague Carol Wallinger (Rutgers-Camden) and her willingness to review the entire book and give me detailed feedback.

I am grateful as well to the innumerable colleagues around the country who constantly "rip and burn" ideas for teaching the course on the LWI Listserv. I cannot imagine a more creative and supportive national community in any field, or one with a stronger sense of sharing and collaboration. It is likely that many of the ideas in this book are derived from things I have learned from discussions on the Listserv over the years. If I have unintentionally borrowed an idea without giving due credit, please let me know and I will give proper credit online and in the next edition of the book. As the great authors of the *Examples & Explanations* book for legal writing noted in their Acknowledgments: "We hope that if we have forgotten to acknowledge an individual, you will understand that after years of teaching in such a generous community we are sometimes no longer sure where each idea originated or how many wonderful colleagues have added to it."**

I am grateful to my former Dean Marty Katz, who has been immeasurably supportive of my work over his 7 years as Dean. And I am deeply indebted to the late former Associate Dean Federico Cheever, my mentor, guide, and friend, who freely offered broad wisdom and boundless patience whenever I needed it. I will miss his insights and wisdom immensely.

I am grateful to the law school, to former Dean Katz and particularly to former Associate Dean for Faculty Scholarship Alan Chen for scholarship support while writing the first edition of this book. I am also grateful to the Institute for the Advancement of the American Legal System (IAALS) at the University of Denver, which appointed me its Visiting Scholar in the spring of 2013. This appointment provided me an office space at IAALS during my sabbatical where I was able to finish this book around congenial and smart colleagues doing good work.

I am indebted to my late father David S. Thomson, a teacher himself and an editor, who suggested many improvements to the first edition of this text.

Finally, I am greatly indebted to my wife Kathy and my daughters Angelina and Sarah-Jane. Kathy has been a wonderful advisor to me over our 20+ years together. I could not be doing this work without her help and counsel. And our daughters support and encourage me in myriad ways—even when they do not know they are doing so—and I appreciate their generosity of spirit (and so much more) about them.

** Terrill Pollman, Judith Stinson, Richard K. Neumann, Jr. & Elizabeth Pollman, *Examples & Explanations: Legal Writing* xi (Aspen, 2012).

Skills & Values: Lawyering Process

Chapter 1

The Lawyering Process

Introduction

By entering law school, you the student have asked your teachers (and textbook authors) to help you become a lawyer. But what does it mean to be a lawyer? And what sort of lawyer do you want to be? It is not too early to start asking yourself these questions. While you may not know the answers yet, thinking about them is a valuable thing to do, even in (perhaps especially in) your first year of law school.

Practicing law is a profession, which means that we—the community of lawyers—profess something together, and we do that publicly (which is what *profess* means). We profess together that we will adhere to a declared and shared set of values, and we agree that we will all act in ways that uphold the rule of law. For lawyers this is expressed in the Code of Professional Conduct. A shared code of values is the *sine qua non* (an indispensable element) of a profession. The preamble to the Model Rules of Professional Conduct captures this well:

> A lawyer, as a member of the legal profession, is a representative of clients, an officer of the legal system and a public citizen having special responsibility for the quality of justice.... A lawyer should use the law's procedures only for legitimate purposes and not to harass or intimidate others. A lawyer should demonstrate respect for the legal system and for those who serve it, including judges, other lawyers and public officials.... Lawyers play a vital role in the preservation of society. The fulfillment of this role requires an understanding by lawyers of their relationship to our legal system. The Rules of Professional Conduct, when properly applied, serve to define that relationship.[1]

So in swearing an oath to uphold the Code (which you will do when you are sworn in as a member of the bar in a few years), lawyers acknowledge that they play a special role in society, and owe a duty to the effective functioning of that society by exercising skill and moral judgment in the performance of their work. Among other things, this means that lawyers are not necessarily supposed to do everything a client asks them to do.

Within those bounds, there is room for you to begin to think about, and eventually decide, what sort of lawyer you want to be. The Code of Professional Responsibility

1. Model Rules of Professional Conduct, Preamble §§1, 5, 13 (1983).

provides a "floor" for conduct, below which a lawyer can be disciplined and perhaps even disbarred. While we need to understand those rules (the subject of another course in law school) we want to dedicate our professional lives to working somewhere above the floor. Where you will operate is part of your own decision as to what sort of lawyer you want to be. We call this the formation of your professional identity.

In short, being a lawyer means you are committed to a set of important duties and responsibilities. It is an important job and intellectually rewarding as well. This book introduces you to the fundamental skills and values that lawyers must have to effectively do their work. Keep in mind, though, that this is only an introduction. One of the great things about deciding to become a lawyer is that you are committing yourself to being a life-long learner of all the skills and values needed to be a professional counselor at law. And it starts now.

What Lawyers Do

What do lawyers actually do? In basic terms, the lawyer's job is to determine the law that applies to a client's situation, to counsel the client about the available lawful options, and to advocate for the client in private meetings and public venues such as courts.

Clients come to lawyers with plans, problems, or issues that involve the law. You might have come to law school thinking that lawyers just "look up the answer" in law books and give that to the client. But it is generally much more complicated. Legal problems rarely have easy answers; if they did, there would not be much need for lawyers. Lawyers do indeed look up the law and find somewhat similar situations to the one the client is involved in. Very rarely, though, do they find the exact same situation. As a consequence of this, lawyers draw analogies and comparisons between the law and the client's situation, and use that information to counsel and represent the client. We use these prior situations and compare them to client facts in an effort to predict or argue a certain outcome on behalf of the client.

The "lawyering process" is the process that lawyers go through to do their jobs and obviously (given the title) it is the subject of this book. It involves legal research skills (looking up the law), reading skills (reading statutes and cases and interpreting them), and legal reasoning skills (drawing analogies). And it involves advocacy skills—representing a client's position to others, in writing or in the spoken word.

All of these skills are essential to becoming a lawyer. You can be an effective lawyer without knowing well certain parts of the law, but you cannot be an effective lawyer if you cannot find the law, read it quickly and competently, draw analogies, and analyze and articulate the situation your client is in, and advocate on behalf of your client to others. While there are many types of lawyers and specializations within the profession, all lawyers must have these fundamental skills. So learning the lawyering process is in many ways the most important part of becoming a lawyer. Time spent learning these fundamental skills in law school will always be time well spent. But remember that it takes time to master them; few students become great legal writers and researchers after one year of law school. The ones who become accomplished legal writers typically do so later in their careers. They are able to achieve this, however, only when they have had a good foundation in law school and have spent time building on that foundation later on in school and in practice.

To be good at the lawyering process you need to learn several discrete things. You need to understand how the American legal system is set up. You need to learn how to conduct legal research so you can find the statutes and cases that are applicable or analogous to your client's situation. You also need to know how to read the statutes and cases that you find and process what you read into useful information for your client. You need to know how to organize what you have found and then present it in writing. You need to know how to write certain legal documents, and understand the audience for those documents. You need to learn and follow accepted legal writing style, and you need to learn the particular form of citation to authority that commonly supports legal writing. You need to learn how to orally advocate for your client's position and how that differs from legal writing skills. The chapters of this book address each of those discrete skills in turn. What follows is a brief introduction to each one.

Legal Research

Like most forms of information subject to being researched, legal material is categorized in a particular way, and interconnects in a particular way as well. Once you learn the categorization scheme, and the methods of interconnection, it becomes easier since they repeat across areas (or subject matters) of the law. For example, state law and federal law are considered separate systems, but they are organized in similar ways so if you learn one you can learn the other more easily.

Today legal research is a more complicated task than it used to be since there are a plethora of sources for legal material. As late as the 1970s legal information was primarily found in the statutes, and in casebooks, treatises, and law reviews—all printed resources housed in libraries. Starting in the 1980s, the two major online research services, Westlaw and Lexis built two computer-based research services roughly parallel to the physical books. In the late 1990s free online services brought legal research resources onto the Internet and these continue to proliferate.

When legal research was limited to printed materials in law libraries, the task of conducting research was similarly circumscribed and straightforward. But today competent legal researchers not only need to know the strengths and weaknesses of each of these sources, printed and electronic, but also how to mix and match them for greatest efficiency. Some research tasks can be started on Google but end in books. Others may need to start in books, move to the paid online legal resources and end with free Internet legal resources. The best way to begin learning how to be an excellent legal researcher is to approach the changing tasks with flexibility and an open mind, and to think of each task as a learning opportunity to expand and hone your research methods.

Reading Legal Materials

At first reading legal material—statutes, cases, and analysis of both—will seem foreign. This is primarily for two reasons: (1) legal material uses many terms that are new to non-lawyers, and (2) legal material is presented in formats that are unfamiliar to non-lawyers. Once you get used to both differences they will no longer seem foreign.

The best ways to get used to these differences is immersion and attack. One of the reasons that first year law school is so difficult—you may feel at times that you have strapped on a firehose—is found in the value of immersion. You are in some senses learning a new language, and as with foreign languages immersion works well for most people. But passive immersion is not the best approach when you are learning how to read legal material. Instead, you want to attack—interact with it, push back. Look things up, ask questions, and write in the margins things like: "what?" "how does that make sense?" and "why was this statute written this way?" Be quizzical.

Case briefing is a technique used by many first year law students as they are reading cases and learning how to interact with legal materials. There are several useful forms of briefing a case. The one that is best is the one that works best for you. But the basic idea behind briefing a case is to break it down into its component parts so you understand what it adds to the law in the area you are studying. By articulating in your own words the issues in the case, its procedural history, the case's holding and its reasoning, you interact with it more deeply and are placed into a quizzical relationship with the court's decision.

Organizing What You Find

As you conduct legal research—reading the statutes and cases you find and taking notes on them—you will discover that you need to develop a method of organizing what you have found. That way you will not need to backtrack on your research and can pick it up again where you left off after taking a break or after working on other projects. There are a number of software programs—many of which are used by law offices across the country—that can help you do this, such as CaseMap from Lexis and Amicus Attorney from Abacus Data Systems. With these programs you can link to the electronic file containing the case, or to statutory material that you may have found online, and take notes on what you found to be the most important or helpful facts or holdings from each case. These programs can also help you to categorize the holdings into groupings that help to express the law in the area. Categorizing what you have found is an essential step in the research phase as you prepare to analyze what you have found and think through how it might apply it to a client's situation.

Basic Legal Documents

Legal writing takes several primary forms. Legal "memos" are typically internal documents, shared only within the law office where you work or with a client, and offer an objective analysis of the law and its applicability to the client's situation. Legal "briefs" are external documents, filed with a court or regulatory agency, and offer an advocacy position in support of a resolution of a legal issue that is favorable to your client. Legal "transactional documents" (such as contracts) memorialize agreements made between two or more parties to exchange goods or services and are typically the result of negotiations between the parties that are facilitated by a lawyer. Lawyers also write many other sorts of documents, such as opinion letters (expressing a legal opinion to a client), demand letters (requesting a resolution of a client matter before litigation), and settlement letters (memorializing or requesting certain terms for settlement of a dispute).

All of these legal documents follow a particular form of legal expression and are written in a similar style. The common form of legal expression is in four parts: (1) a statement of the issue or concern, (2) an explanation of the legal rules that are applicable to that issue, (3) an application of the rule to a client's facts, and (4) a conclusion that summarizes the explanation and application provided. If there is more than one issue needed to fully analyze the client's problem, this form is repeated to address each issue in turn.

Legal Writing Style

The style of legal writing, or its tone, is not informal, but it is also not turgid and full of legalese. Despite what you may have thought before law school, important sounding terms such as "wherefore" are frowned upon in legal writing. But legal writing does have its conventions. For example, contractions and idiomatic or slang terms are frowned upon. The highest value of legal writing is being concise and to the point. Writing that is plain, simple, and direct is what you aim for. This is for good reason: the topics lawyers write about are usually rather complicated so making the complicated simple is what is most valued. While these rules might at first seem constraining, there remain many opportunities to be creative. The avant-garde jazz bass player Charles Mingus put it best: "Making the simple complicated is commonplace; making the complicated simple, awesomely simple, that's creative."[2] Filling up your writing with frills or misdirection will just distract your readers from what they need to understand: the law as it applies to your client.

To achieve this sort of simple and concise writing requires a different sort of approach than what you might have used in prior writing experiences. It requires much more planning and time in the pre-writing stages. Starting to write without any pre-planning is a recipe for wasting time and a poor final product. Writing with insufficient pre-planning is also inefficient, hampering your efforts and making the process more difficult than necessary. A simple outline—which might have worked for you in the past—will usually not be sufficient to help you produce a good piece of legal writing. Rather, a "thick" outline with detailed instructions to yourself about which section

2. Olivia Bertagnolli, *Creativity and the Writing Process* 182 (1982).

will discuss which case, and what parts of that case will be emphasized in that section, is what you need to prepare before you start writing. If you spend the time doing that sort of work in advance, the final product will always benefit because it is much easier to write plain, simple, and direct prose when you understand the problem thoroughly and know exactly what comes next in your explanation of it.

The best lawyers are meticulous about the writing they produce, and invest considerable effort into making sure each document conveys what it needs to, and that it does so in the least amount of space. They are careful to assure the accuracy of their citations to authority, and they proofread their documents closely. These efforts all contribute to the reputation and authority of an attorney. A strong reputation is one of the best ways to get new client referrals so it is worth developing good habits now, and putting in the extra effort to edit and proofread your documents with a high attention to detail.

Citation

The key to understanding legal citation is that it is designed to provide the reader with all needed information about the authority you are offering for a particular statement in your writing, while also taking up the smallest possible amount of space. It is important to be proficient at it since it validates your writing while providing valuable information concisely. It can certainly seem picky and difficult as you are learning it. But if you are careless with your citations, you not only miss opportunities to provide important information, but you also undermine your credibility as a lawyer. Your fellow lawyers and judges expect citations to be in the correct form. When they find citations that are sloppy, missing, or incorrect they immediately question the care the writer has taken with the rest of the product, whether it be a memo, letter, or brief. If the citations are poor the analysis is assumed to be poor as well. Good citation and good writing complement and support each other; you cannot have one without the other.

Advocacy

Lawyers of all types are advocates in one way or another, not just the trial lawyers that you see on television who embody the archetype of the lawyer-advocate. All lawyers advocate for their clients' needs and interests. Often they do so out of the public eye, in negotiations or in drafting agreements. Sometimes they advocate for their clients in court, trial, or in appellate argument. In any of these settings, advocacy involves the skills of persuading others that your client's position is the one that should prevail. So an essential component of being a lawyer is being an advocate.

Often the advocacy work lawyers do is not in writing exclusively, but is conducted orally—in speech—in either private or public settings. So a key aspect of what lawyers do is express legal information on behalf of a client through the spoken word. Thus, part of the lawyering process is developing the skills of oral advocacy, the ability to speak clearly, concisely, and effectively on behalf of a client.

This might be something you welcome, or something you find daunting. Even if you welcome it you will find it more challenging that you might at first expect. It is hard to learn to express legal information in a way that is clear and convincing and yet not histrionic. If you find it daunting, learning the basic skills of oral advocacy and practicing them will help make you more comfortable. At a minimum it will give you the confidence to complete the task required and do so with aplomb. The Lawyering Process course usually ends with training in oral advocacy and provides opportunities to practice it and learn its component skills.

Conclusion

So this is what lawyers do. They learn about a client's problem, research the applicable law, and apply it to the client's situation in writing and orally. It is good and important work, and an honorable profession to join. In this quote Teddy Roosevelt reminds us why: "Far and away the best prize that life has to offer is the chance to work hard at work worth doing." You will find, I suspect, that studying law and practicing it will offer you *work worth doing* in copious amounts.

Further Reading

Ian Gallacher, *Coming to Law School: How to Prepare Yourself for the Next Three Years* (Carolina, 2010).

Michael Hunter Schwartz, *Expert Learning for Law Students* (Carolina Academic Press, 2008).

Exercise

Prepare a self-assessment of your past writing experience in accordance with the instructions provided by your professor.

As You Prepare This Assignment, Consider the Following

Why did you decide to come to law school and what do you plan to do with your degree?

What type of reading, writing, research, and advocacy have you completed prior to law school?

How do you anticipate these skills translating to law school and your future law career?

What are your writing, researching, and speaking strengths? Weaknesses?

ONLINE: Your professor will provide the self-assessment assignment and an example.

Chapter 2

Legal Work

Introduction

While some law school graduates start their own legal practice immediately upon graduation, this is relatively rare. It is far more common for graduates of law schools—once they have taken and passed the bar examination—to be hired to work in a law office of some type. As you begin your legal studies, it is helpful to think about the available options for your first job, and to understand the sort of work you are preparing yourself to do. This chapter describes the most common types of law offices and the sort of work that is done in each.

As recently as 40 years ago private law firms hired most graduates of law schools. There they acted in effect as apprentices, and were not paid very much until they matured as attorneys and were able to take on their own clients, or help significantly with work for clients the firm already represented. Eventually they became partners in the firm with management oversight responsibilities and a share of the firm's profits. There was little movement from firm to firm.

Over the last several decades much of this system has changed. With that change has come some advantages and some disadvantages. On the good side, as the market for legal work has expanded, more varied opportunities for law school graduates have opened up. Among these are work in district attorney offices, public defender offices, a broad array of judicial clerkships, work with non-profit institutions, government agency work, and more opportunities to become involved in international legal work. On the not so good side, economic pressures have made the old apprenticeship model virtually extinct, surviving only in a few of the largest law firms, and even there in a more limited way than before. Law offices now expect new hires will be ready to operate effectively much sooner than in the past. If they are not ready when they start working they may not keep their job. On the good side again, there is often more variation and mobility in a typical young lawyer's career than in the past. Young lawyers today change jobs more often than they used to. Their first job will not likely be the same one they hold down later in their careers.

In all law offices, lawyers who are looking to hire a new law school graduate are usually quite clear that in addition to good character and a willingness to work hard, what they most need in a new lawyer are the skills of legal research, writing, drafting, and citation. As a result, the subject of this course—the fundamental skills that all lawyers need to practice law—while always important, has only become more so. There is every reason to think this will continue to be the case in the future.

Law Offices

These fundamental skills will always be vital but the particular sorts of writing recent graduates might be asked to do will vary depending on the type of law primarily practiced in the offices where they work. A young lawyer who joins a small practice focusing on criminal matters will likely be writing motion briefs, appellate briefs, and arguing simple motions in court. If instead the graduate joins a personal injury law firm, she is likely to be involved in the discovery phase of litigation—obtaining information on cases from opposing counsel and providing the same in return. This often involves motion briefs as well, research memos, demand and settlement letters, and occasionally an appellate brief. By contrast, a recent graduate who joins a corporate in-house counsel's office will be involved in reviewing and drafting contracts, conducting research on regulatory provisions that affect the company, and preparing or reviewing settlement agreements. A young lawyer who joins a small family law practice is likely to be meeting with clients fairly soon and will be preparing mediation statements, petitions, and property division and child custody agreements. A lawyer who joins a real estate practice as a new attorney will likely be conducting legal and property research, preparing memos, and drafting transactional documents. A government agency lawyer might find himself drafting or reviewing proposed legislation, reviewing contracts, or discussing regulatory requirements with enforcement staff. An attorney joining a civil rights firm might be drafting appellate briefs more than is typical in other practice areas.

The common denominator for all these legal jobs is writing skills. There is no other way to put it: lawyers write. If you hate writing and everything connected with it, you might want to reconsider law school. It is even important to *becoming* a lawyer: half of the bar examination is writing answers to essay questions. Writing is important to many jobs, of course, but it is essential to being a lawyer.

The Importance of Self-Care

Many students come to law school hoping to help others solve problems. This is a good and laudable goal, and a great and joyful reason for attending law school. Without lawyers willing to help their clients, our society would be in worse shape than it already is. But this responsibility and this work comes with burdens.

Clients do not generally bring lawyers easy problems. They bring the hard ones, the ones they are not able to resolve without help and guidance. These problems can be very difficult and usually have high importance for the client. It is essential to remember that the work you are doing might have drastic consequences for your client; it is *their* job at stake, *their* ability to protect their child, perhaps *their* freedom or financial well-being. As a direct result of the importance of the work that lawyers do, it is often hard to maintain balance in legal practice. Lawyers often work extra hours to get the work done and sometimes forget to take proper care of themselves, or give that a lower priority. Lawyers have a high rate of stress and dissatisfaction in practice, and substance abuse is not uncommon.

It is not too early therefore to begin to develop methods of self-care so that you can handle the pressures of law school (now) and law practice (later). A primary thing to consider is this: how have you managed stress before you came to law school? Regular exercise is known to help manage stress. If that is a part of your life now you are encouraged to keep it up. If it is going to the movies or to a museum, you are encouraged to keep that outlet, too, and nurture it. There are pressures in law school to excel and it is easy to push off self-care to another day while you focus on your studies. But that approach risks laying down a poor foundation for practice that will catch up with you later. It would be better to try to find balance while you are still in law school. You are encouraged to make stress management part of your work routine now so it will stay with you and you can become a contented and healthy lawyer ready to take on the toughest of client problems.

One important aspect of self-care is finishing your research and written projects on time and not procrastinating up to the deadline. This is a good habit to start in law school and maintain throughout your law career. Completing your work ahead of time will help not only to produce quality work and establish a positive reputation with colleagues and judges, but also help to lower stress levels and help you to find balance.

Further Reading

Stefan H. Krieger & Richard K. Neuman, Jr., *Essential Lawyering Skills* (4th Ed., Wolters Kluwer, 2011).

Lisa Penland & Melissa H. Weresh, *Professionalism in the Real World* (NITA, 2009).

Exercise

Interview a practicing lawyer either in person or on the telephone. Ask them what they do each day, the role that research and writing plays in their practice, and ask them to describe an ethical dilemma they have faced recently. After the interview write a memo describing the attorney's practice, what you learned from the interview, and reflect on how it made you think about what it means to be a lawyer.

As You Prepare This Assignment, Consider the Following

Who did you decide to interview?

How did you find that attorney?

Was the attorney welcoming of the interview, or not so welcoming?

What does the attorney do in the regular course of her job?

How do they conduct legal research, and what sorts of documents do they write?

Does their work sound interesting to you, or not so much?

What ethical dilemma did they describe to you?

Did you think they handled the ethical dilemma properly, or did it make you uncomfortable?

What do they do to get away from the office, or to take care of themselves or their families?

How did interviewing the attorney make you feel about your decision to attend law school?

ONLINE: An Example Memo for this exercise. You will also find articles about law practice, links to job postings, and information about career choices.

Chapter 3

The Legal System

Introduction

As you begin to learn the law it is essential to have a basic understanding of the legal system and how it operates. For many first year law students some of this chapter may seem like a refresher from a 10th grade civics class. But if you do not know these basics the first few months of law school will be much harder and more confusing than they need to be. Even for those who feel they already know this information a quick review will be helpful.

How the American Legal System Is Designed

Our legal system is made up of laws and regulations, with judges writing opinions interpreting the meaning of them. There is a Federal system of laws and cases, and one for each State. There are also local ordinances at the level of the city or municipality, and cases that interpret those as well.

Federal statutes come from the United States Congress and State statutes from state legislatures while local ordinances come from city governments. Some statutes establish specific requirements or limitations by themselves, and some create agencies that issue regulations that do the same (and some do both). An example of a Federal statute is the Americans with Disabilities Act (ADA), which establishes rules for the accommodation of persons with disabilities in public places (such as movie theatres) across the country. The ADA also empowers an agency (in the case of the ADA, the Department of Justice) to promulgate regulations offering more specific detail than is provided in the statute, and to enforce the requirements of the law and the regulations. An example of a state statute is one that establishes a psychiatrist's duty to warn of a dangerous patient making specific threats of violence against specific persons. An example of a city ordinance is one that sets limits for noise after certain hours and empowers a local policeman to issue a summons to a late night college party that got too loud.

All of these statutes and ordinances are subject to compliance or resistance. A business might voluntarily comply (as many have) with the ADA by installing a wheelchair access ramp. But that business might also legitimately believe that the wheelchair access ramp requirement does not apply to it. That resistance might cause an enforcement action, which would then either be resolved or end up in court. In the state statute example, the psychiatrist might decide that the threshold for the duty to warn did not apply to a particular patient—only to find that the patient has caused harm to others. This matter might well end up in court. In the local example, the college student hosting the party might decide that the policeman did not have sufficient grounds to issue the summons and decide to go to court to dispute the charge.

It might be tempting to think that legislation can address all situations and thus not require the courts to interpret them, but the reverse is true. In reality, legislators cannot predict all the eventualities that will arise in the application of the statute they have issued. As the British philosopher Isaiah Berlin believed, the "crooked timber of humanity"[3] is too varied and too unpredictable. Imperfection and unpredictability is a reality of human society and always will be. But the fact that laws will always require interpretation and application is to be welcomed by a law student since this is the work of lawyers and provides jobs for new ones. If practicing law were as uncomplicated as applying clear statutory provisions to simple client situations there would be far less need for attorneys than there is.

Both criminal matters and civil matters arise from statutes. Criminal matters are what you frequently see playing out in television shows and movies. These involve the adjudication of guilt or innocence for a particular violation of a statute. They are overseen by a judge but usually decided by a jury. Civil matters are everything else, such as a contract dispute between two companies doing business with each other, or whether a business needs to comply with the ADA. Some civil matters are tried by a judge alone without help of a jury.

When a dispute arises that ends up in court it is usually heard first in a trial court. The trial might result in several sorts of rulings on evidentiary or discovery matters as well as the final ruling about guilt or innocence of a defendant, or whether a business needs to install an ADA-approved wheelchair ramp. Often the trial involves both issues of "law" and issues of "fact." That is, there may be a question about what the law is that applies, and a question of what the facts are that underlie the case. Any of these rulings may result in a written opinion from the judge, but this is particularly true of rulings that relate to how the applicable statutory provision should be interpreted when applied to the set of facts before the court. That written opinion becomes a "precedent" and is then available for future criminal defendants, litigants, attorneys, and judges to use to discern what the law is or should be when applied to a different set of facts.

In both the federal system and the state systems, trial court rulings are subject to review by a court of appeals. These are courts that just hear appeals; they do not try cases but instead are tasked with fixing any mistakes that might have occurred at the trial level. The judges hearing the appeals also issue opinions, which also become precedent. Court of appeals rulings are in turn subject to further appeals, to the state

3. *See* Isaiah Berlin, *The Crooked Timber of Humanity* (1998). The title of Berlin's book comes from a quote of the German philosopher Immanuel Kant: "Out of timber so crooked as that from which man is made nothing entirely straight can be built."

supreme court for a state matter, and to the United States Supreme Court for a federal matter.[4]

This process leads to the principle of *stare decisis*, which is Latin for "to stand by things decided." This fundamental principle in our legal system ensures consistency and reliability in the law, and is based on a hierarchy of authority. Under *stare decisis*, prior case law is either mandatory or persuasive. Mandatory authority (also called "binding authority") is that of a court higher than the one where the same question of law is being considered. Persuasive authority is that of the same or a lower court as the one where your client matter is currently active. There is also an occasional crossover between federal court decisions and state decisions. In federal decisions that interpret and apply state law, those precedents are only persuasive for state courts, even though you might think of the federal court as being the "higher" court.

In sum, an opinion from a supreme court is more authoritative than an opinion from a court of appeals. An opinion from a court of appeals is more authoritative than an opinion from a trial court. Indeed, for a trial court, an opinion on a matter of law from either the state's court of appeals or the supreme court is considered binding on the trial court. It is important, then, that when your client matter is in a trial court, or the court of appeals, and there is no decision of a court of appeals on a particular point of law, that you determine whether there is a supreme court opinion on the same or a similar point. If so, the supreme court opinion would be the one you would rely on as the mandatory authority. But this does not mean that decisions of lower courts are not helpful to higher courts. To a court of appeals, the decision of a trial court—if it were the only decision on the question of law available—might still be persuasive authority for the court. This is also true of an opinion from the court of appeals—or even the Supreme Court—in another State. It is through the principle of *stare decisis* that the law grows and develops through a series of opinions in which statutory provisions are applied to case facts.

Although *stare decisis* is essential to our legal system, a court can overrule its own prior opinions. The United States Supreme Court has done this many times over its history, particularly in matters of interpretation of the U.S. Constitution. In the words of Supreme Court Justice Stanley Reed: "[W]hen convinced of former error, this Court has never felt constrained to follow precedent. In constitutional questions, where correction depends upon amendment, and not upon legislative action, this Court throughout its history has freely exercised its power to reexamine the basis of its constitutional decisions."[5]

When reaching a decision courts will often rely on more than just primary authority, which is the applicable statute and prior opinions interpreting that statute.

---

4. There are occasions when a question of state law is appealable to the United States Supreme Court, and occasions when a state law matter might end up in federal trial court, but these are addressed in your Civil Procedure class, as well as in other law school classes, and are beyond the scope of this introductory discussion.

5. *Smith v. Allwright*, 321 U.S. 649, 665 (1944).

They also occasionally rely on what is called secondary authority, or at least consult it. Secondary authority is legal commentary and analysis, in the form of treatises (books) on the particular area of law, or law review articles analyzing the law in the area, or a Restatement (summary) of the law in an applicable area. Secondary authority is only persuasive authority (never mandatory), and the level of its persuasive value is determined by the weight given to it by the judge writing the opinion in the case that assesses the relevance of the authority and the reputation of its source.

Administrative agencies with enforcement and adjudicatory authority also issue opinions. These can be helpful when your client has a matter before that agency, and can provide guidance on how a regulation issued by that agency has been applied in the past to other parties. Should the dispute between the client and the agency come to court, these agency opinions can have persuasive authority in the courts. So it is particularly important when handling such a matter that you make sure you understand the agency precedent as well as any court precedent that has addressed the client issue.

It should be clear by now that statutes and precedents are critical in our legal system, and you will need to build the myriad skills of legal research to find them, and the particular skill of reading cases and statutes to interpret them. The next two chapters address these skills.

Further Reading

Karl Llewellyn, *The Bramble Bush: The Classic Lectures on the Law and Law School* (Oxford, 2008).

Jay M. Feinman, *Law 101: Everything You Need to Know About American Law* (Oxford, 2010).

Exercise

Access online the New York Burglary Statute, and prepare an outline of the statute in which you express its component parts. Show how the statute is designed, and to what sorts of situations it applies.

As You Prepare This Assignment, Consider the Following

What are the elements of this statute?

What different considerations must be met for a person and action to be included within the purview of this statute?

Can you think of a set of facts that would clearly be a violation of this statute?

A set of facts that would not be a violation of this statute?

A set of facts where it could go either way?

ONLINE: An example statutory outline for you to consult as you complete this assignment.

Chapter 4

Reading the Law

"Good lawyers are good readers."[6]

Introduction

One of the most important qualities an excellent lawyer should possess is the ability to efficiently read large volumes of complex material with a high level of comprehension. You may have come to law school thinking yourself a good and competent reader and you probably are. Most law students excelled in prior stages of their schooling and this likely also required a high level of reading ability. But the level of reading in law school and in practice is of a magnitude greater than you are probably used to, and at first it also involves understanding things about the law that you do not know yet. So you are entering an era in your education that involves immersion in a flood of information, and much of it will seem at first as if it is in a foreign language. The first few weeks of law school can thus seem overwhelming and you may feel as though you are walking around in a fog. Understanding the common forms and methods that you will find in legal authority (statutes and cases) will help you get your bearings.

Reading Statutes

When reading statutes, it is good to think of an onion and a telescope. With an onion, you need to slice it to use it, or separate it into its component layers. With a telescope, you can focus in on particular crater on the moon, or zoom out to focus on the moon as a whole. To understand a statute fully, you need to do both: break it down, look at it closely, and also zoom out to look at the whole thing.

Usually you do not need to read a statute like a book, from beginning to end. Rather, you find the specific provision embedded somewhere in the statute that applies to your client's situation. Then you break down the specific provision and determine the elements of the statute that apply to your client, including any exceptions. The best method of doing that is to outline the provision as you did in the assignment after Chapter 3. For example, taking the Colorado dog bite statute,[7] for a plaintiff to bring suit against the owner of a dog that bit her, a required element is "serious bodily

6. Laurel Currie Oates & Anne Enquist, *Just Memos* 97 (3d ed. 2011).
7. Colo. Rev. Stat. § 13-21-124 (2017).

injury" and there are several exceptions to this rule. Breaking down a statute (or section of a statute) into its component parts is a critical step in reading and understanding all statutory provisions.

There is, though, another required step. You have found the specific provision that is most important to your client and the temptation is to focus on just that provision. Instead you need to take time to look at the statute as a whole, to take the long view of it. Often statutes will begin with statements of purpose and intent in which the drafters will have expressed the problem the legislature was trying to address.[8] An expression of legislative intent can be quite helpful for putting specific provisions in context. Definitions of key terms used throughout the statute—which you might find embedded in it, located at the beginning of the statute, or defined in another statute—can also be useful. Looking at the dog bite statute as a whole reveals that the term "serious bodily injury" is, in this case, defined in another statute. While this is fairly obvious in the dog bite statute, in a longer or more complex statute such a critical cross-reference would be easy to miss.

Breaking down the statutory "onion" into its component layers will help you see the design of the statutory provision and its operational aspects. Zooming out to view the statute as a whole will help you see its overall purpose and intent as well as to find definitions of key terms. Both techniques will help you read and comprehend statutory material more quickly and efficiently.

Some statutes are clearly written and have a straightforward meaning. Other statutes may be unclear or ambiguous and leave you wondering in what situations the legislature intended the statute to be applied. When reading an ambiguous statute, you may want to turn to the canons of statutory construction for guidance, since a judge might use these tools to interpret legislative intent. Canons of construction are principles that provide guidance to courts when they are interpreting ambiguous statutory language. For example, the canon of construction *noscitur a sociis* (which means "it is known from its associates") suggests that words grouped in a list should be given a related meaning. *Ejusdem generis* (which means "of the same kind") is another canon which suggests that when a general term follows a list of specific terms, the general term should be read to apply only to other terms that are analogous to the specific terms it follows.

Reading Cases

However, even after all these efforts, statutory provisions alone rarely provide a complete or exact answer to the client's problem. And while terms used in the statute may be defined within the statute, those definitions rarely answer the client's problem

8. Also, examining legislative history for the statute—comments made by legislators at the time the statute was being developed and passed—can be helpful in understanding its purpose and intent, although the value of legislative history is often a subject of dispute. As a matter of legal research, how to find the legislative history for a statute is addressed in Chapter 5.

either, and sometimes they may even make it *less* clear whether a provision applies to your client. Also, terms are often left undefined in statutes.

Sometimes, there is no statutory provision that applies to your client's situation at all. Significant areas of law are not statute-based, but instead are known as *common law*, or "judge made" law. These legal doctrines arose from a string of cases—sometimes over many years and perhaps even dating back to old English common law—that established a legal principle, and has been refined since.

For all these reasons (and sometimes in combination), we must look to the other form of primary authority to assess the client's situation, and that is case law. Cases, expressed in judicial opinions—a written decision from a court—apply statutory language (or a common law principle) to a specific set of facts that are before the court in a pending case. While you will find much variation in the cases you read over the course of your career, most judicial opinions follow a particular pattern.

First, there will be a statement of the legal issue (or issues) of law before the court. Then the court provides a recitation of the facts of the case, which is usually followed by a statement of the applicable law. Then a discussion of the law as applied to the facts, which is usually followed by a holding of the court (the *decision*) and then the reasoning behind the decision will be provided.

In cases where a panel of several judges is adjudicating the case—as in a court of appeals or a supreme court—the decision is often anything but unanimous. Some of the judges will have one view of the case, the others the contrary view. When they have taken a vote the majority view wins. Thus, you can have not just a "majority decision" but along with it a "minority opinion" or "dissenting opinion" in the same case. The majority decision, of course, becomes the law, but a minority opinion can be persuasive enough to affect future thinking on the issue—and sometimes a dissenting opinion can as well. Sometimes with large panels of judges, several members of the majority will issue what is known as a "concurring opinion," which contains further thoughts expanding on and buttressing the majority decision. These concurring opinions may also influence later judicial thinking, and usually have greater persuasive power than minority opinions, and both generally have greater influence than a dissenting opinion.

Occasionally as part of a court's decision a judge will offer an opinion about how the law should be interpreted in the future, should certain facts differ from the facts of the particular case before the court. This is known as *obiter dicta*, which is Latin for "things said by the way." Not considered part of the court's holding in the matter before it, *dicta* has persuasive authority only. But it can occasionally be useful in understanding the underlying legal principle, and in making an argument about how the law should be applied in the somewhat different situation described in the case, which might be more similar to your client's situation than the precedent itself.

Be wary of cases that apply an earlier version of the statute that you are analyzing. Be sure that the language the court is applying is exactly the same as the language in the current version. If it is not, you will want to consider that potential issue in your analysis, in particular whether the difference is material or not, and whether later cases have applied the current language in the same way as the prior case.

As you read cases, you are naturally looking for similarities and differences between the facts of the case and your client facts. If the facts are similar, you might be able to rely on the case as a guide to how the law will be applied to your client's issue. Even if the facts are different, though, the case may still have value for your analysis since sometimes—as in life—it is helpful to know what the result will *not* be.

Case Briefing

Lawyers write case briefs—short summaries of cases they have read—because they read cases and need to understand them, and briefing helps them do that. Briefing a case is a form of taking notes, which are most helpful when they follow a particular format; the format helps when referencing your notes later. Case briefing helps you "process" the material you are reading, rather than having it wash over you in a wall of words. The format you use should be one that works best for you; there is no single perfect format for briefing a case. But, it certainly should include a concise statement of the issue, a list of the key facts, the law that was applied, the holding, and a note or two about the court's reasoning. You might also—if it is important to the court's holding—include the procedural history of the case, that is, a brief description of the steps the case took in the legal system before it came to the court that issued the opinion. This processing of a case is about finding, and being able to articulate, the *rule of law* from the court's opinion. The *rule* from the case is found in the holding and reasoning, as applied to specific statutory requirements or common law principles in the case, under the facts before the court.

When you read cases and write briefs, you should keep in mind that judges are fallible people just like everyone else. Sometimes you will come across a case that is very difficult to read or understand. This might be because the law being addressed is particularly complicated. It also might be simply because the judge produced a poorly written opinion. Do not be afraid to be critical of the cases you read. As you read and brief them, interact with them. Write in the margins things that do not make sense to you. Question what went on in the case, and think about whether you think the decision was correctly decided. Ask yourself questions like, "Who were these people?" and, "Who really did what to whom?" Make the case your own. Take charge of it.

Synthesizing Several Cases

As noted, it is rare for a statute to solve a client's problem, but it is also rare for one case to solve it. Indeed one rarely finds a case that is an exact match with your client's facts. And so we need to read and brief multiple cases in the same area of the law to begin to understand how the law might be applied to the specific client's situation. This requirement was perhaps best expressed by the noted law professor Karl Llewellyn who said: "... a case read by itself is meaningless, is nil, is blank, is blah.

Briefing should begin *at the earliest* with the second case of an assignment. Only *after* you have read the second case have you any idea what to do with the first."[9]

If statutory language alone does not solve the client's problem, and if one case does not, it is reasonable to wonder how several cases would help. But it is exactly here that the heart of lawyering lies. Since statutory language does not directly apply to the exact situation the client is in, and there is no case exactly on point, then what lawyers do is try to predict what will (or should) happen in this new situation, one that has never happened exactly like this before.

Having done this work, the lawyer will have a pretty clear idea of the most likely outcome of the client's case. In the next chapter you will be introduced to the basic concepts of legal research—how to find the statutory language and case law that interprets it—so that you may make these predictions based on what you find as applied to your client's facts.

Further Reading

Ruth Ann McKinney, *Reading Like a Lawyer: Time-Saving Strategies for Reading Law Like an Expert* (Carolina Academic Press, 2005).

David S. Romantz & Kathleen Elliott Vinson, *Legal Analysis: The Fundamental Skill* (Carolina Academic Press, 1998).

9. Karl Llewellyn, *The Bramble Bush: The Classic Lectures on the Law and Law School* 52. (Oxford, 2008) (emphasis in original).

Exercise

Read the *Leichliter* case (available online), and prepare a case brief for it.

As You Prepare This Assignment, Consider the Following

What are the material facts of the case?

What happened, and to whom?

What are the procedural facts of the case?

What steps have been taken by the parties and courts to resolve this case?

What is the legal issue or question the court is being asked to resolve?

How does the court answer this question?

What is the Rule of Law established by this case?

What reasoning does the court provide?

Do you agree with the court's decision?

ONLINE: A link to the *Leichliter* case, and an example case brief.

Chapter 5

Legal Research

Introduction

When a client comes to seek your help with a legal problem they will tell their story and often bring documents with them. Depending on the type of case, they may bring you a summons, hospital bills, contracts, letters, receipts, or witness statements that, put together, will establish the facts of the case. Your responsibility is to determine, and later persuade a judge, how the law applies to the particular set of facts. How the law applies to the facts becomes your legal question. You will need to research which statute might relate to your client's case and how the court has interpreted that statute to apply to similar factual circumstances. Without an ability to find the relevant law it would be hard to be an effective attorney. For this reason, becoming an expert at conducting legal research is a fundamental lawyering skill.

Developing a Research Strategy

The best way to start any research project is to generate search terms by making a list of terms and phrases related to your legal question. A legal dictionary or thesaurus can assist you in developing search terms. As you delve into your research project, expand upon this list as you are introduced to new terms. While you are learning how to conduct research, getting started can be the hardest part. Some law students find using the acronym TARP to be a helpful guide. To use the TARP approach, you will extract from your client facts the following elements and use them to guide your initial research: Things and places (for example: baseball, ballpark), cause of Action (injury), Relief sought (damages), and Persons or Parties (child, baseball fan).

A good next step is to familiarize yourself generally with the applicable area of law. This can include searching for your topic in secondary sources found online or in the library. Once you establish a general understanding of the area of law, you will want to locate, read, and analyze primary authority in the applicable jurisdiction. As you know, primary authority includes statutes, case law, and administrative regulations. You can search for relevant primary sources using online databases or printed finding aids in the law library. In order to analyze the statutes or cases you have found, you may need to rely on secondary sources or locate additional case law.

Finally, once you have located relevant primary sources, you need to make sure the authority you have found is still good law—that a statute has not been amended or revoked, or that a case has not been overturned or remanded. It is important to develop the habit of always updating the primary material you have found.

Types of Legal Research

Primary and secondary legal material can be found in books located in law libraries, from free online sources, and through paid online databases. There are advantages and disadvantages to each of these research methods.

Going to the library gives you free access to all of the materials the library subscribes to, and the assistance of reference librarians. The downsides of library research are that it might be inconvenient to travel to the library, and it might take a good deal of time to flip through the books. In an increasingly online world, you might be dismissive or even fearful of the library. Take advantage of your school's law library while you are still a law student and take time to explore the books. Putting your hands on these sources will improve your online research skills by increasing your understanding of what sort of legal information each source contains and how the sources interconnect with one another.

A natural place to start any research project is Google or another online search engine. A great benefit to searching on Google is convenience and, of course, the cost is free. In your law practice, as you specialize in certain areas of law, you will become familiar with the free online sources that are used and trusted by lawyers in your field. Ask your mentors what sources they use. Google Scholar can be a terrific free source for case law, and works well if you already know the name of a particular case you are seeking. For any lawyer, your state's judicial and legislative websites can be useful (and free) sources for cases and statutes or for pending legislation. Also, state agency websites are a good place to search for their governing regulations. The disadvantage of using free online sources is that it is difficult to know when your research is complete. Not all the information that might be helpful to your research question may be available through free online search engines. Also the credibility of the source, or your certainty about whether it is current, can be a concern.

You are probably already familiar with the traditional subscription online databases, Lexis and Westlaw, and perhaps one of the newcomers such as Bloomberg Law. These databases provide access to both primary and secondary sources, are convenient, and are linked to additional sources. The great strength of the paid online databases is that you can be confident that they are credible and current. The disadvantage to these databases is the cost. Most law practices do not subscribe to the broad levels of access that you enjoy as a law student. Because research fees—sometimes charged by each search and result—are usually passed on to the client, it is important to be prudent in developing a research strategy and to perform database research as cost-effectively as possible.

Any competent legal researcher uses a combined method that adjusts for the type of research in question. For example, as a law clerk, the attorney you are working for might give you an assignment that asks you to research the duties of a children's ombudsman. Having never heard the term before, you Google "ombudsman" and learn that an ombudsman is an independent and impartial advocate. You also find a link to your state's children's ombudsman website and a national ombudsman association. Next you use one of the online legal databases such as LexisNexis or Westlaw and find your state's child ombudsman statute within the Children's Code. You also see that the state has a set of regulations governing the ombudsman, but unfortunately your subscription does not cover this type of legal source. You check the state's website which is, unfortunately, "under construction," so you go to the law library to find and copy the regulations. A law clerk with a mix of those sorts of varied research skills, and who knows when to use each type of resource, is a valuable new employee in any law office.

Sources of Law and Legal Information

Primary Sources

Attorneys use primary legal sources to determine what law exists and what law will apply to the set of facts at hand. Primary sources consist of material from all three branches of government. The legislative branch creates laws that are organized by subject and published in statute books. The judicial branch issues opinions, or case law, which is organized into case reporters, or books of sequentially published cases. The executive branch (such as an agency) issues regulations designed to interpret, extend, or enforce the laws passed by the legislative branch. Regulations are organized by subject into sets called codes. Statutes, cases, and regulations can all be found both at a law library and through paid online databases. Increasingly, these sources can also be found online at each state's judicial, legislative, and executive branch websites.

Statutes. The federal government and each of the 50 states have an official set of statutes and may additionally have unofficial sets. A statute citation generally follows the formula: Title-Article-Section. A set of statutes generally has multiple indexes, which allow a legal researcher to find relevant statutes by topic, popular names, and/or words and phrases. Each statute will include what is called a source note, which will explain the legislative history of the statute. In addition, the statute is generally accompanied by annotations designed to point the researcher to other primary and secondary sources that will interpret or explain the statute. These annotations are a valuable source through which you can find related case law. Because statutes are constantly being amended or replaced, it is important to make sure you are looking at the most recent version of the statute, or the version of the statute that applies to the timeframe of your case.

Case Law. Case law is organized into case reporters from a particular jurisdiction or geographical area. Reporters are a series of books that contain cases that are published sequentially by their decision date, not by their subject. West has developed a National Reporter System that organizes cases into state and federal court reporter sets. Select Federal District cases are in a set of reporters called the Federal Supplement (F. Supp.). Appellate cases from the 13 Federal Circuit Courts are found in a set of reporters called the Federal Reporter (F.). U.S. Supreme Court Cases are found in the United States Reporter (U.S.). State appellate court and Supreme Court cases are published in one of seven regional reporters: Atlantic Reporter (A.), North Eastern Reporter (N.E.), North Western Reporter (N.W.), Pacific Reporter (P.), Southern Reporter (So.), South Eastern Reporter (S.E.), and the South Western Reporter (S.W.). Some states may also publish cases in individual state reporters, or online as part of the public domain.

A case citation reads Volume, Reporter and Series, then page number. For example, to locate the case 126 P.3d 196, 126 is the volume number indicated on the spine, P.3d is the Reporter (Pacific) and Series (3d), and 196 is the page number where the first page of the case can be found.

Using West's case reporters you will be introduced to West's Topic and Keynote System, which is used across all of West's primary and secondary sources, both online and in print, to help you identify and organize useful and related information. In the case reporters (and on Westlaw) before the text of the opinion, you will find a list of headnotes. Each headnote contains a Topic and Key Number followed by a brief explanation of related information from the case at hand. You can use these headnotes to gain a general understanding of the law covered in the case. Locate the headnote number within the opinion text to learn what the court has said about the topic. The LexisNexis online database has a different headnote system, but it works in much the same way.

Secondary Sources

Attorneys use secondary sources when researching an unfamiliar area of the law. They use such resources to help find, understand, and interpret primary legal material. The information you have when you are beginning your research project will help to determine what secondary sources will be most useful to you. Secondary sources may be broken down into finding aids/updating sources and explanatory sources.

Finding Aids/Updating Sources

Case digests. Case digests are a set of indexes, which provide point of law summaries and cites to relevant cases. West's Digests are organized by West Topic and Key Number system. Digests are set up by geographic region or jurisdiction. For example, each of West's geographic reporters has a corresponding case digest. You might already have a Topic and Key Number from another West publication or you can search for a relevant Topic using the digest's corresponding Descriptive Word Index, Table of Cases, or Words and Phrases volume.

Shepards. *Shepards* is a Lexis publication that helps you to update your cases. Updating cases is important to ensure that the cases you have found are still good case law, and have not been reversed or overruled by a higher court. Most legal researchers use an online legal database to update case law instead of using the print edition of *Shepards*. You can also use *Shepards* as a finding aid to locate related cases that mention the case you have found, follow it, distinguish from it, or disagree with it. These additional sources may help to fill in your research.

Explanatory Sources

Legal dictionaries. These are useful for finding definitions of legal terms and locating additional search terms to use when researching. Black's Law Dictionary uses West's Topic and Key Numbers to help locate on-topic information in other West publications.

American Law Reports. These contain entries called annotations. Each annotation is like an extended law review article that interprets selective cases and discusses points of law. The A.L.R. state volumes currently has six series. There is also a federal series. You can find a relevant A.L.R. annotation using the General Index, Table of Cases, West's A.L.R. Digest, or Table of Laws Rules and Regulations. Once you find an annotation series, use the Table of Contents, Research References, and the Table of Cases all found at the beginning of each annotation to quickly find useful information.

Legal periodicals. These are publications on specific legal issues written by experts in the area and are a good source to find relevant primary sources and other secondary sources. Most law schools produce one or more law journals. In addition, state bar associations generally publish a legal periodical. ***Legal periodical indexes***, as well as LexisNexis and Westlaw, can assist you in finding relevant articles. Three noteworthy indexes are the Index to Legal Periodicals, LegalTrac, and HeinOnline, all of which you can probably access through your library's website. Often these indexes will link you to the full article online.

Legal encyclopedias. American Jurisprudence and *Corpus Juris Secundum* are legal encyclopedias published by West. Both encyclopedias contain discussions of hundreds of legal areas and are extensively footnoted to provide case citations from different jurisdictions. A legal encyclopedia is a good place to familiarize yourself with a new topic. There are also online encyclopedias that can provide a general background.

Treatises and hornbooks. These are commentaries designed to interpret the law and are prepared by experts in the field. When using these sources be sure to pay attention to the footnotes, which are often packed with information about related cases and statutes.

Restatements. Restatements are published by the American Law Institute to codify specific areas of common law reflecting current and emerging trends. There are Restatements for many areas of law such as the Restatement of Torts and the Restatement of Contracts.

Practice materials. These are generally jurisdiction-focused and written by local, experienced practitioners; they provide analysis, commentary, and practical tips for practicing in the area of law in your jurisdiction. Practice materials usually provide attorneys with best practice standards and sample court documents.

Legislative History

Legislative history material, which comes in various forms, can help interpret a statute by giving insight into congressional intent when the statute was passed. A statute in a codebook or online database includes a source note, which details the public law numbers, the date of the original legislation, and the dates of any amending legislation. The next step is to locate these various pieces of legislation that have formed the statute. Once a legislative act is enacted into law, the text of the law is assigned a public law number and published in the United States Statutes at Large and the U.S. Code Congressional and Administrative News (USCCA). Valuable legislative materials may accompany the public law, including committee reports, legislative hearings, and floor debates, all of which might help you determine congressional intent. For federal legislation enacted after 1970, an excellent legislative finding aid is the Congressional Information Service, which you can find online. Another is THOMAS—the online information service of the Library of Congress. Some states have similar systems, or you may have to contact the legislature's library to help locate other supporting information. A librarian at your law school can help as well.

Interpreting and Using the Authority You Have Found

Controlling vs. Persuasive Authority

Look back at the discussion of mandatory vs. persuasive authority in Chapter Three. It is important to keep the difference in mind when conducting legal research. When you find a useful source, ask yourself: Is this controlling or persuasive? Particularly when researching case law, you want to begin your research in the controlling jurisdiction. Only mandatory sources are controlling in any given case before a court. A judge will look to statutes and regulations as well as controlling case law when deciding how the law applies to a particular case.

Secondary sources, legislative material, and primary sources from other jurisdictions are occasionally used as persuasive authority. These materials can be used to reinforce an analysis discussed in the controlling authority or to let the court know how other jurisdictions have interpreted the same or similar law in factually analogous situations in their jurisdiction. Persuasive material can be particularly useful when there is limited controlling authority in your own jurisdiction on the point of law you are researching.

Good or Bad Case Law

An important step with any legal research project is to update the case to determine if the case still has precedential value. Updating case law is known as shepardizing a case. Shepards is a Lexis service, but Westlaw offers a similar system called KeyCite. The case heading will contain a green, yellow, or red flag (Westlaw) or a symbol (LexisNexis). A indicator denotes that the case is still good case law, or has received positive treatment. A yellow indicator denotes that you should proceed with caution because there is possible negative treatment. This might indicate that a subsequent case found a different application of the law, but the facts of that case might distinguish that court's reasoning from the case you are researching. A red indicator marks negative treatment of the case, which usually means that the case is no longer good case law and you should not use it to answer your legal question. However, be careful in automatically dismissing cases that have subsequent negative treatment: the negative treatment might concern a topic that is covered in the subsequent case, but this is not a topic that concerns the issue you are researching. In that situation, the case might still be useful to you if it remains good law on the topic you are researching.

Unpublished Opinions

Most cases decided by a court lead to a written opinion finding facts and expressing a holding; however, courts and judges do not publish all of their opinions. A judge may choose not to publish an opinion because the case is perceived by the judge to lack precedential value. As a result, when conducting your research you might stumble upon unpublished cases, particularly when searching online. Generally, you should not rely on unpublished opinions for support. Unpublished opinions can be used as persuasive authority, but primarily when there is no other authority available on the legal question being discussed.

Contrary Opinions

As an advocate for your client, it might be your first instinct to only present to the court case law that is favorable to your client. However, it is important to also present to the court contrary opinions and in many situations there is an ethical obligation to do so. Because the court will most likely conduct its own research, and the opposing counsel will likely present a case that is unfavorable to your client, it is often your best strategy to inform the court of the existing contrary case law, and then explain why your case is different from this contrary opinion, by distinguishing the two.

Tracking Your Research

Organization is key to any successful research project. Keep track of your search terms, and the sources you have located in folders provided by the online legal research services. CaseMap, a LexisNexis database software designed for attorneys, can help here, as can an Excel chart, or another organizational system that works best for you. A good organizational system should be easy to navigate, not only for the research question at hand, but also for a similar research question that might come along later. Keep track of the date you located each source, and always remember to update your research.

When to Stop Researching

When learning how to conduct legal research, it is difficult to know when to stop. It is natural to worry that there may be something you are missing, and so the tendency is to want to keep looking. But you need to balance the research phase with the analysis phase in any project. Sensing when to stop researching and begin analyzing what you have found, and writing about it, is an important skill to learn.

Fortunately, there is a good method that should help. You can generally trust that you are nearing the end of your research project when you find yourself reading a new case in the area and you find that you are already familiar with all the on-topic cases the court discusses within the opinion *as well as* with all of the cases cited when you shepardize the case. Put more simply, you can stop researching when the cases you are finding all start citing cases you have already read. Then, when you have gathered and organized all of the relevant authority, the next step in answering your legal question is to develop a synthesized rule statement explaining the legal principle that will apply to your client's legal problem. This lawyering skill is addressed in the next chapter.

Further Reading

Amy E. Sloan, *Basic Legal Research: Tools and Strategies* (5th ed. Wolters Kluwer, 2012).

Mark K. Osbeck, *Impeccable Research: A Concise Guide to Mastering Legal Research Skills* (West, 2010).

Exercise

Conduct the research necessary for the fall semester memorandum assignment, following the instructions of your professor.

As You Prepare This Assignment, Consider the Following

What are the primary sources you will need to find to understand what law applies to your client's situation?

What secondary sources will you use to help understand and interpret the primary sources?

How did you know when it was time to stop researching?

Which indicators show that you have found all of the cases relevant to your client's legal issue?

How are you going to organize the information you have found?

What if you discover research that may be detrimental to your client, what will your approach to that situation be?

ONLINE: Library Pathfinder exercises, Tutorials, online research problems, and MindMaps of research results.

Chapter 6

Legal Memos

Introduction

A common way to express the application of relevant legal principles to client facts is in the form of a legal research memorandum (or a "legal memo"). This is a specialized form of writing that follows a specific format. It is objective in tone, describing the law as it applies to a client and is not an advocacy document that seeks to persuade. It is an internal document—internal to the law office representing the client—and thus is never submitted to a court or shared with opposing counsel. It is often assigned to a junior attorney by a senior attorney in the office, and this is done when the senior attorney needs to understand better how the law applies to the client's situation. It is often used by the senior attorney to counsel the client about her options going forward.

Lawyers write memos, and ask junior attorneys to write memos, as a way to carefully analyze the state of the applicable law so that an appropriate decision can be made about how to proceed. These memos take considerable time to research and write and as economic pressures increase on law offices some are viewing the traditional memo as increasingly time-consuming and expensive. Even so, learning how to write a traditional legal memo remains useful for two reasons: (1) the skills you learn in writing a full-length memo are easily applied to any research assignment that is shorter than that, and (2) if you are asked to write a full-length memo you will be able to do so.

As with all writing, it is important when writing a legal memo to know your audience. Think of the audience for your memo—the senior attorney who gave you the assignment to write it—as a non-specialist in the particular area of law. This attorney may know (for example) landlord-tenant law quite well but not be fully familiar with the specific provision your memo addresses. So you want to tailor your memo with that in mind, by minimizing the general discussion of the broad legal area and focusing instead on the specific particulars of the case.

This book presents the basic and most common format for a legal memo. Some senior attorneys may have specific preferences that differ from this format in minor ways. Fortunately, understanding how to write the full memo makes the component skills adjustable to any situation or preference.

The IRAC Format

The most common format for a legal analysis is expressed in the acronym IRAC. The letters in the acronym stand for: **I**ssue, **R**ule, **A**pplication, **C**onclusion.

In this format, the writer expresses the legal **I**ssue at hand, then describes the **R**ule of law that pertains to the issue, then **A**pplies the rule of law to the client facts, and then **C**oncludes. More briefly, the form is: state the issue, explain the rule, apply the rule, conclude.[10] Most lawyers reading your memo will expect this basic sequence, so you should use it.

In virtually all legal expression it is expected that the author will start with the general rule and move to the specific. So it is normal in the rule section of an IRAC to have a general rule stated first, which is then followed by a more specific rule that applies to the particular situation at hand.

There are variations to the IRAC format but they all amount to basically the same approach. One variant is expressed in the acronym CREAC. According to this approach your analysis should take the form of: **C**onclusion, **R**ule statement, rule **E**xplanation, **A**pplication, and **C**onclusion. That is, you should highlight the conclusion up-front and then restate it at the end. Whichever format your professor suggests is the one to use for now. When writing for a senior attorney in a law office you should of course use the format he or she prefers. But the differences between them are fairly subtle; once you have learned one format, adjusting to the others is easy. The goal is always to write a sound and sufficiently complete analysis, not one that rigidly follows a specific format.

The IRAC form may seem foreign to you at first and constraining. But it should not—the IRAC form is common in many settings. To first state the problem, then how the problem has been addressed in the past, then how that approach would or would not work in a specific new circumstance, and to then conclude, is a common way to frame any argument. Once you learn the form and it becomes part of how you think, you will realize that it is not limited to the law. Indeed, you will start to see it everywhere, in news commentary, in political speeches, and even in the sports pages.

Synthesis

The rule of law you express in IRAC is not usually a rule drawn from just one case. Rather, it is a rule, expressed in your own words, in which you have summarized the holdings from several cases. This is known as a synthesized rule of law. It is the opposite of a list of case holdings: "Case A held this, Case B held this ..." Rather, it is a statement of what the holdings in several related cases all add up to. An example

10. The two middle parts of IRAC are the longer and more complex of the four. Those middle parts are sometimes expressed, for clarity, as **R**ule **E**xplanation and **R**ule **A**pplication.

of a synthesized rule of law is: "When use of disputed land has been open and notorious, and the property has been in continuous use by the claimant, courts have held that ..."

To develop your synthesized rule of law, try this. First, rank your authorities by hierarchy. Second, look for similarities among the cases. Are there several cases that reach essentially the same result under different facts? Group those holdings into a "bucket." Third, look for differences among the cases. Are there a few cases that reach the opposite result under certain common (but different) facts? Group those into another "bucket." Finally, express the common themes (and distinguish the differences) in one sentence. Here is another example of a synthesized rule statement: "In determining whether a statutory duty to warn exists, the courts consider two main factors: whether a specific threat was made, and whether a specific person was named in the threat."

Basic Format of a Legal Research Memo

Legal research memos follow a particular format, with some variation. As with the IRAC form, the variation is minor and once you learn one format you can easily adjust to a different one. This book follows the Question Presented, Brief Answer, Statement of Facts, Discussion, and Conclusion format. These sections of the memo are discussed below.

Question Presented

The Question Presented (QP) is where you express the question you were asked, and the one that you address in the memo. A good way to draft the QP is to follow the **Under, Does/Is/Can, When** formula. The way this formula works is: **Under** refers to the applicable law, **Does/Is/Can** refers to the legal issue, and what follows **When** are the key determinative facts of the client's problem that are the most important to answering the question. Here is an example of a QP following that format:

> **Under** the Colorado Trade Secret Act, **is** a customer list a trade secret **when** its access was limited to two people, was password-protected, but contained valuable competitive information?

Brief Answer

The Brief Answer (BA) is where you provide a response to the QP. You may provide a definite Yes or a definite No to the question, and you may also provide a qualified answer. If you provide a qualified answer, you want to explain why the answer should be qualified. Here is an example of a BA that might follow the QP above: "Yes. The customer list is a trade secret because it was only accessible by our client and the Company's CEO, was located on a password-protected computer, and it included customer survey data which contained detailed information about customer preferences."

Statement of Facts

The Statement of Facts (SOF) in a legal research memo should be short and concise but provide sufficient factual information about the client's situation to support the analysis provide in the memo. When you were given the information about the client situation you might have been given a lot of detail. Yet when you started to research the matter you might discover that only a portion of the facts you were given are important to answering the QP. As much as possible, you should include in the SOF only the relevant facts and ignore the rest. Other facts would be those that are unimportant and are not determinative of the question you were asked, so there is little reason to include them in your SOF.

One way to sift the important facts from the non-important ones while you are drafting your memo is to write the SOF later in the process. Just because these various elements of a memo are presented in this order does not mean you have to draft them that way. Indeed, it is often easier to draft a concise SOF after you have written most of the rest of the memo, and have a better understanding of the key facts that need to be included in the SOF. Generally you should not have a fact in the SOF that you do not reference in the discussion section of your memo, and you should not have a fact in your discussion section that is not introduced in the SOF. An exception is when you need to include an extra fact in the SOF simply to provide some context or background needed to make the client's story easier to understand.

Discussion Section

The discussion section is the heart of a legal research memo. It is where the relevant legal rules are fully explained, and where they are applied to the client's facts. Within the format of a discussion section there can be some variations, but this book suggests that you include an overview paragraph at the beginning of the discussion section and thesis paragraphs for each sub-section.

An overview paragraph, also called a "roadmap" paragraph, lays out the key legal principles and briefly applies them to the client facts. It follows the same organization as the discussion that follows it. It usually cites to the applicable statutory language, but does not otherwise cite case law, since citing to case law is reserved for the rule explanation paragraphs later in the discussion section of your memo.

Legal research memos often address more than a single legal issue, but even if they only address one, they usually require a multi-step analysis on that issue. That is, you need to break down your analysis into several logical steps. An example of this would be a legal principle that uses a two-factor analysis. In such an example, the legal rule requires that two factual elements be present for the legal principle to apply. If one or more are lacking, then the principle does not apply to the situation.

You present this sort of multi-step analysis in the form of subsections in your discussion section, one for each step. Each sub-section of your discussion will address one step of the analysis. Usually you begin with a heading that indicates the subject of the sub-section. The sub-section then begins with a thesis paragraph, which is then followed by one IRAC that addresses this step of the analysis. This is followed by another subsection in the same form that addresses the next step of the analysis.

A thesis paragraph should be quite short and provide a very brief roadmap for the analysis step that is the subject of the sub-section that follows. A good formula for a thesis paragraph is to provide one sentence on the rule of law that applies to the particular sub-section and a following sentence that briefly applies it to the client's situation.

A new paragraph usually starts with the IRAC form. In it, you state the issue in one sentence, and then you launch into the rule explanation, going from general to specific, and provide illustrations from the relevant cases. As you introduce a case, you should start with key facts from that case, then explain or provide the court's holding, then provide the court's reasoning. As you draft a rule explanation it is helpful to focus on the parts of the facts, holdings, and reasoning from the precedent case that you will use in your rule application to make comparisons to your client's case. You want those two parts of the IRAC form (rule and application) to be as parallel as you can make them, in detail as well as length. In the rule application paragraph, you want to make as many direct fact-to-fact comparisons as you can between the precedent case and the client's case. It is on those detailed comparisons that the strength of your analysis rests. Once you have constructed the IRACs for your memo you will be able to see how it would be helpful to then go back to the statement of facts to make sure you have included all of the facts that you need for your rule applications in each IRAC.

It is important to keep rule explanation and rule application sections separate from each other, usually in separate paragraphs. Explaining a part of a rule while trying to apply it, or applying it while trying to explain it, can be confusing to your reader, and it is not the form they are expecting you to use. Mixing the rule explanation and rule application is known as "blendering," and you want to avoid doing that. It is also important to keep the two sections as balanced (in length) as possible. Ideally, the Rule Explanation section will describe specific elements of the rule, and these same elements will line up with the Rule Application section that follows it.

When encountering the IRAC form for the first time it is tempting to view it as a set of requirements that must be stated in only one way. But it is better to think of IRAC as an accordion that can be flexibly expanded or contracted to most effectively address the simplicity or complexity of the legal question being addressed. Thus, it is possible that a complex legal issue would require a form more like IRRAAC, since there might be two closely related rules that would benefit from being treated somewhat separately from each other (and applied separately as well). Or you might decide that the legal principle you are describing would benefit from an IRARAC form where the two sub-rules are less closely related to each other but still belong in the same sub-section.

The Conclusion

The conclusion section of your memo comes last and is often written last as well. It should be a simple summary of the key legal rules that apply, and of the key determinative facts that resolve the question you were asked to address in your memo. It should be a standalone item that can be read by itself to get the full sense of your memo, what it covers, and what decision you reached in conducting your research. Because it is often read first, it should be especially clear and self-sufficient, giving the gist of your analysis to the senior attorney who asked you to write the memo.

That is quite enough exposition about the legal research memo form. The best thing to do next is read sample memos that are available in the online companion site for this book and write practice research memos that have been assigned by your professor. You should not expect writing a legal research memo to be something that you can master in one try. It is only learned through an iterative process, by trying and making mistakes and receiving feedback from your professor and then trying again. You should also not expect to be an advanced memo writer at the end of the first year of law school. These are skills best learned over time, to be cultivated and expanded upon through the rest of your years in law school, and indeed throughout your legal career.

Email Memos

As noted at the beginning of this chapter, some law offices are reducing their reliance on the full legal research memo and moving instead toward shorter forms of communication. Among these is the email memo, which essentially summarizes the results of legal research in the form of an email. Often the request will come to the junior attorney in the form of an email with a deadline provided.

Even so, an email memo should take the same professional tone as a full memo, should answer each legal question presented, and should provide an IRAC-based analysis that states the legal rules, cites key cases, and applies the rules to the client's facts. Think of an email memo as using many of the same techniques as a full research memo but doing so in a more abbreviated form.

Oral Report

Your senior attorney may also request an oral presentation of what you found while conducting research on the client's problem. If asked to make such a presentation, you first need to understand that this is not an opportunity to simply read your memo (or draft memo). It is more of a conversation, but a fairly formal one, in which you explain the cases you have found, and draw analogies and comparisons between the facts of those cases and the client facts of your case (much as you do in the memo). Generally you will not need to recite the facts of the case. Instead you will want to focus on the substance of your research. You want to be careful to not assume the senior attorney wants a particular result. Instead just objectively explain what you have learned in your research. The senior attorney will likely ask for your conclusion on the question and you should offer it. If your conclusion is qualified, or not definite, then you should expect your senior attorney to want to delve into the details of what is non-determinative in the law, and how your legal analysis might change depending on any additional facts that might come to light as your firm's representation of the client proceeds.

Further Reading

Laurel Currie Oates & Anne Enquist, *Just Memos* (4th ed., Wolters Kluwer, 2014).

Cassandra L. Hill & Katherine T. Vukadin, *Legal Analysis: 100 Exercises for Mastery, Practice for Every Law Student* (LexisNexis, 2012).

Exercises

(1) Draft a memo addressing the problem materials provided by your professor.

(2) Respond to the Senior Partner Assignments (email memo assignments) as your professor assigns them.

(3) Prepare an oral report to a volunteer attorney or your Professor about the results of your research.

As You Prepare This Assignment, Consider the Following

What is the legal question at hand?

What facts are essential to answering the legal question?

Have you begun your discussion section with an overview paragraph?

Does each subsection begin with a thesis statement?

What statutes and cases govern your client's situation?

How does this authority apply to your client's facts?

Have you clearly separated your rule explanation from your rule application?

How have you incorporated contrary cases into your memo?

What information will your senior partner want to know when you meet to discuss your research and analysis?

ONLINE: Example memos and checklists, as well as information about the oral report assignment.

Chapter 7

Legal Citation

Introduction

A crucial element of a good legal document is its authority. Writers of legal memos and briefs lend authority to their work through citing case precedent and other sources. As an attorney, you will give validity and strength to your legal documents in part by citing case precedent and other legal sources. Each authority has a citation, so that you may inform the court, other attorneys, or other readers where to find the material you reference. This chapter addresses the importance of citation, when to cite, and how to cite the most common sources used in memos and briefs in the first year of legal writing. This chapter addresses the basics of citation form according to the most common form of citation, known as the "Bluebook."

What Is the *Bluebook*?

The *Bluebook* sets out the rules for uniform legal citation. It is maintained by the student editors of the law reviews of Harvard, Yale, Columbia, and the University of Pennsylvania. Every few years they reconsider the *Bluebook* rules and publish a new edition with (usually) minor changes. Many of the more arcane rules pertain to law review citation, not practitioner citation. Most first year courses focus on the practitioner citation rules in the *Bluebook*.

Why We Cite

Uniformity in legal citation is necessary for practitioners, judges, and scholars to easily find and investigate the sources cited. As strange as the *Bluebook* may seem when you first open it, there is logic to its design. Its rules prescribe that publication information be in a pattern that leaves a trail of breadcrumbs, so to speak, for the reader to follow to the precise location within a source where you found your information. For example, the order of a case citation, at a minimum, shows the reader the name of the case, the reporter (book) it is in, on what page the case can be found, the precise page on which the specific quote or idea used by the author is located, and in which court and the date the case was decided. In a citation, in one brief sentence, the reader is concisely provided valuable location information as well as information about whether the case is binding or persuasive.

Citation is a reliable code that leads the reader to the authoritative source of the law. Practitioners and judges expect accurate citations from attorneys so that those authorities can be reviewed and verified. Accuracy in your citation shows the reader your attention to detail and bolsters the strength of your position. A citation also properly attributes a thought, idea, or doctrine to its original author or source. Correct and precise citation is the surest way in practice of signaling to the reader your honesty, integrity, and reliability. Providing accurate citations is a vital way to build your professional reputation and to portray professionalism in your communications with colleagues, opposing counsel, and courts.

When to Cite

Legal practitioners most commonly cite when:

- Referencing the facts of a case;
- Referencing the holding(s) of a case;
- Quoting directly from a case, statute, or other source;
- Using or expanding on another author's ideas; and
- When synthesizing a legal rule derived from several cases

The general rule is, when in doubt, cite. At the end of this chapter there is a brief exercise illustrating key principles of when to cite. There are additional exercises online.

Using the *Bluebook*

The *Bluebook* may seem overwhelming at first. Here are a few tips to keep in mind when using the manual. First and foremost, do not try to memorize the *Bluebook*. It is a reference guide of more than 500 pages and one that undergoes updates and revisions every few years. It would be wasted time and energy to memorize all the rules and every nuance and exception to them. It is a reference manual.

Second, when you are writing your memos or briefs keep the *Bluebook* on your desk so that you can check the citations as you put them in your document. You should do this even if you think you have correctly memorized the citation format for a case or statute.

Third, even if you do not put the full citation for a rule or idea in your first draft, at least mark the locations where you need the citation and include the source name and page number. This will save you time and frustration when you begin to finalize your document with complete citations.

Key Elements of the *Bluebook*

The *Bluebook* begins with blue pages, which are followed by white pages, which are followed by pages that are white with blue trim. The Bluepages contain summarized citation rules that govern memo and brief writing. The fonts, rules for underlining, and other style details in the Bluepages are the formats you should follow when writing your briefs and memos in your first year legal writing course, unless otherwise instructed by your professor.

The Whitepages supplement the Bluepages with more detailed rules for the authorities mentioned in the Bluepages and rules for additional sources. The font and stylization in the Whitepages should not appear in a memo or brief. The stylization provided in the Whitepages is for law review articles, books, and footnotes. The general rule is that all words italicized in the Whitepages should be underlined in a memo or brief. Any words appearing in small caps in the Whitepages should be in a regular font in a memo or brief. The tables are printed on white paper with blue trim at the end of the manual; they include citation formats for individual states and abbreviations necessary for citation of cases, journals, and other sources.

The outside back cover of the *Bluebook* provides a quick reference guide for law students and practitioners looking to locate a specific rule. The back cover gives the page and rule number for each source of authority in the *Bluebook*. For example, statutes are governed by Rule 12.

Inside the front cover are general formats for the most common sources; these formats are in the typeface and stylization for law review articles and footnotes (Whitepages). Inside the back cover is the same information, but in the typeface and stylization for memos and briefs (Bluepages).

The Index

Possibly the most helpful feature of the *Bluebook*, the index is a 30-page catalogue of nearly every type of source one might cite in a legal document, and it provides the page number for the rule that governs citation for that source. In addition, the index includes common names of sources so that the practitioner does not have to be precise in attempting to find the governing rule. Lastly, *Bluebook* users can look up problems with citations and quotations in the index in order to find out how to indicate the problem in a citation.

- Note: Words or phrases in blue indicate that the word or phrase actually appears in the citation. For example "available at" or "*id.*"

The Tables

The *Bluebook*'s tables are found in the back of the manual and are a crucial tool for making correct citations. The tables interact with the *Bluebook* rules; rules will specifically reference a table when it is needed to fill in necessary information in a citation. For example:

- In Rule 10.2.2. the reader is directed to Tables T6 and T10 to find out how to correctly abbreviate words and geographic locations in case names referenced in a citation sentence.

- Note: Carefully read the introductory paragraph to T6, which explains how to make an abbreviated word plural. However, if the word has alternate endings shown in brackets [ ], then the abbreviation is good for each of those words.
- Another example: Rule 12.3 directs you to T1.3 in order to find the correct format for the official and unofficial statutory code for each state and U.S. Territory (states and territories are listed alphabetically in T1.3). Thus, if you wish to cite a Colorado statute, the student should look in T1.3 for the jurisdiction of Colorado to find the correct format for statutory citation and the preferred source.

Cross-References

In addition to the tables, the rules may refer you to other portions of the *Bluebook* that are important in making a citation. As mentioned above, Rules 10.2.2 and 12.3 cross-reference the relevant tables. All cross-references to other rules or tables will appear in blue bold type. Here are some other examples of important cross-references:

- Rule 16.2 governing names of authors in the citation of journal articles and other periodicals refers you to Rule 15.1, which governs the citation of authors of books or other non-periodicals. This cross-reference is important because otherwise the reader would not know how to form a citation with multiple authors or institutional authors for a journal article.
- Rule 10.2.1(c) governing the abbreviation of words in a textual citation of a case refers you to Rule 6.1(b), which governs the use of acronyms in citations.

Tabbing the *Bluebook*

As you can see from these brief examples, and as will become more apparent as you use the *Bluebook* more, creating a correct citation requires a lot of flipping around between sections of the *Bluebook*. To speed the process and make the *Bluebook* your own it is a good idea to add tabs to it for quick access. Find some sticky tabs at your local office supply store. A list of recommended sections to tab is found online, but at a minimum, you should tab the sections that you find yourself using most frequently. The sections that will be discussed in this chapter include:

- Bluepage Cases, Rule B10
- Bluepage Statutes, Rules, and Regulations, Rule B12
- Court Documents, B17
- Court Document Abbreviations, Table BT1
- *Id.*, R4.1
- Quotations and Alterations, R5
- Case Names, R10
- Short Forms for Cases, R10.9

- Statutes, R12
- Short Forms for Statutes, R.12.10
- Legislative Materials, R13
- Periodical Materials (i.e. Law Reviews and Journals), R16
- Internet Sources, R18
- Your State's Jurisdiction Page in T1
- T6
- Journal Abbreviations, T13
- The Index

Formula for a Basic Case Citation

General Format: <*Case Name*>, V <Reporter> Pa, Pi (<Court/Jurisdiction> <Date>).

- V is the volume of the Reporter
- Pa is the first page on which the case appears within the Reporter
- Pi is the page on which the information the author is citing can be found. This is called a pincite. **Always** include a pincite even if the information is found on the first page of the case so that attorneys and judges will know precisely where to find the information they need.

Case Names: Rules B10.1 and R10.2.1

Rules B10.1 and R10.2.1 govern citing a case within the text of your sentence. Within this sentence a full citation for a case is given and words in the case name **are not** abbreviated according to T6 and T10. The only words that should be abbreviated when you cite a case within the text of a sentence are the eight words found in 10.2.1(c) and the widely known acronyms found in Rule 6.1(b) (FBI, CIA, AARP, etc.). For example:

- In Brown v. Board of Education of Topeka, 347 U.S. 483, 495 (1954), the Supreme Court ruled that the principle known as "separate but equal" is inherently unequal.

Case Names: Rule 10.2.2

In contrast to B4.1.1 and 10.2.1, if you cite a case in a separate citation sentence rather than within the text of the memo or brief itself, the case name will be further abbreviated according to T6 and T10. These case names are created with all the details required by Rule 10.2.1, with the addition of some further abbreviations. For example:

- The Supreme Court has ruled that separation on the basis of race is unconstitutional and the principle known as "separate but equal" is inherently unequal. Brown v. Bd. of Educ. of Topeka, 347 U.S. 483, 495 (1954).

The key difference between citations within your text and separate citation sentences is abbreviation: only abbreviate the words in Rule 10.2.1 in textual citations but abbreviate all possible words according to T6 and T10 in a citation sentence. The reason for this difference mostly lies in aesthetics and the flow of your legal writing. Citations can be distracting to a reader and the goal of not abbreviating a citation within the text of a sentence is to stream the citation into the flow of the sentence as seamlessly as possible. Placing a citation within a sentence disrupts the flow to some extent and abbreviations would further disrupt it. Abbreviations in the citation sentence do not have this effect because a citation sentence is used primarily as a directional signal to the cited authority.

Case Reporters: Rules B10.1.2 & R10.3

The Reporter information of a case citation tells the reader where to go to find the case. Remember, the general format is V(olume) <Reporter> Pa(ge), Pi(ncite). The key to citing to a Reporter is to know which Reporter to cite, since most cases can be found in multiple Reporters. The answer is found in Table T1.3. Table T1.3 indicates which reporters you should cite for the decisions of state courts. For example:

- To cite a case from Indiana, the Indiana jurisdiction table found in T1.3 indicates that for state supreme court and state appellate court cases, cite to N.E. and N.E.2d if therein. This language indicates that an author should cite to these Reporters whenever possible.
- Thus,

  Loparex, LLC v. MPI Release Techs., LLC, 954 N.E.2d 449, 452 (Ind. 2011).

Court, Jurisdiction, and Date: Rules B10.1.3, R10.4 & R10.5

In order to clue your reader in to the jurisdiction and relative authority of the case you are citing, the citation should include where the case was decided and the level of the court deciding the case. The court, jurisdiction, and date are located at the end of the citation in parentheses. The general format is (<Court/Jurisdiction> <Date>).

If you are citing a U.S. Supreme Court case there is no need to include the jurisdiction because it is clear from the reporter. Similarly if you are citing a state case where the jurisdiction is also clear from the reporter, the jurisdiction should not be included. Examples:

- Citizens United v. Fed. Election Comm'n, 130 S. Ct. 876, 880 (2010). The court and jurisdiction is not included in the date parenthetical because it is clear from the Reporter that the case was decided by the United States Supreme Court.
- In re Thomas M., 401 N.Y.S.2d 752, 753 (App. Div. 1978). "N.Y." is not included in the jurisdiction portion of the citation because it is clear from the reporter (N.Y.S.) that the state in which the case was heard in New York.

When citing to a state Supreme Court opinion, unless the state is clear from the name of the preferred reporter listed in T1.3, include the state's abbreviation, found in T1.3 or T10, in the date parenthetical. For example:

- State v. Hughes, 261 P.3d 1067, 1069 (Nev. 2011). Because the citation in this example is to the Pacific Reporter, the state must be included in the parenthetical. By having just the state abbreviation in the parenthetical the citation signals to the reader that the case was decided in Nevada's highest court.

For state appellate court decisions, refer to T1.3 to find out how the particular state abbreviates its appellate court. For example:

- If you are citing a case from the state of Washington, T1.3 indicates that the appellate court is abbreviated as Wash. Ct. App. For example:

  Mansour v. King Cnty., 128 P.3d 1241, 1242 (Wash. Ct. App. 2006).

Similarly for a Federal Circuit Court you abbreviate the circuit in the date parenthetical. Circuit court numbers are abbreviated in the usual way with the exception of the Second Circuit, which is abbreviated 2d Cir., as opposed to 2nd Cir., and the Third Circuit, which is abbreviated 3d Cir. Also, these numbers should **never** be expressed with a superscript font. For example: 10th not 10th. Like this:

- United States v. Black, 369 F.3d 1171, 1171 (10th Cir. 2004).

Lastly, for Federal District Court opinions, abbreviate District as D. and then follow with the state abbreviation for that district. If the district has a geographical prefix, such as Southern, North, etc., abbreviate the directions according to T6. For example:

- Kent v. Lane, 432 F.3d 2000, 2003 (D. Colo. 2012).
- Razzano v. Cnty. of Nassau, 765 F. Supp. 2d 176, 180 (E.D.N.Y. 2011).

Short Case Citation: Rules B10.2 & R10.9

After you have given a full citation of the case with all the required information, you need not continue to cite the case in full. You can now abbreviate the citation to a "short cite." Use the following steps:

- Shorten the first party's name to something that the reader will easily be able to link to the full citation. For example: Brown for Brown v. Bd. of Educ. of Topeka.
- Follow the name with a comma and indicate the volume and Reporter, and then,
- Indicate the page number on which the information or idea you are citing can be found by including "at <page number>" and end the citation with a period. Like this:
- Brown, 347 U.S. at 360.

Formula for a Statute Citation

State Statutes: Rules B12.1 & R12.3

For state statutes, simply follow the formula for the statute given in Table T1.3 for that state and replace the "x" with the appropriate numbers for the statutory provision you are citing. For example:

- The statute format for North Carolina is N.C. Gen. Stat. § x-x (<year>). (The "§" symbol means "section.")
- Thus,

  N.C. Gen. Stat. § 1-2 (2011).

Unnamed Federal Statute: Rule 12.1

General format: <Vol.> U.S.C. § X (<year>).

The trick to this format is that the year can only be in multiples of 6 if you are citing to the print version of the U.S.C., the official code. Since the most recent version is the current year, cite the United States Code like this:

- 28 U.S.C. § 1412 (2015).

As you know, however, Congress changes and modifies statutes all the time. To indicate that you are citing to a statute modified after the print version was published, use the following format:

- If you are looking at updated statutes on Westlaw's online version of United States Code Annotated:
  - <Vol.> U.S.C.A. § X (West <year>).
  - 28 U.S.C.A. § 1412 (West 2016).
- If you are looking at the updated statutes on LexisNexis's online version of United States Code Service:
  - <Vol.> U.S.C.S. § X (LexisNexis <year>).
  - 28 U.S.C.S. §1412 (LexisNexis 2016).

To cite a named act, follow this general format: <Name of Act>, <Vol.> U.S.C. §§ X–Y (<year>). Where X and Y are the first and last sections of the act, annotate thus:

- Americans with Disabilities Act of 1990, 42 U.S.C. §§ 12101–12213 (2016).
- Note: There are two section symbols in this citation "§§ " because the Act covers more than one section in Volume 42. According to Rule 3.3, when citing to more than one section or paragraph of a statute, you use two section or paragraph symbols.

Short Statute Citations: Rules B12.2 & R12.10

Just as with case law citations, once you have cited to a statute in full you can then abbreviate the citation. See R.12.10 for a complete list of short citations.

If you are citing to only one statute in your memo or brief, or if you cite to several statutes but the citations are so different in format that the reader will not be confused, simply cite to the section number and end with a period. Take, for example, the statutory citation to the ADA:

- Americans with Disabilities Act of 1990, 42 U.S.C. §§ 12101–12213 (2016), becomes
  - § 12101.

- Similarly, N.C. Gen. Stat. § 1-2 becomes
  - § 1-2.

However if paring down the citation to just the section numbers would confuse the reader, omit the name of the act and the date for the short citation but leave the rest.

- 42 U.S.C. § 12101.
- N.C. Gen. Stat. § 1-2.

Id.: The Ultimate Short Form Citation

Id. is a short form of citation that is used to signal to the reader that the newly cited statement is attributed to the same source as the immediately preceding authority, whether it be a statute, case, journal article, or other type of source. In other words, *id.* is a shortcut for both you and your reader and *should* be used when you cite the same authority for multiple citations in a row.

Here are some style points to keep in mind when using id.

- Id. is always ended with a period and, if a pincite is needed, a second period is put at the end of the pincite.
- Both the word "id" and its period are underlined.
- If id. begins a citation sentence, use a capital "I"; if not, use lowercase.

For the complete rules that apply to using id., see B4 and Rule 4.1. Below is a pneumonic device ("DOE") that may help you remember the three basic guidelines for using id.

> **D:** does the preceding authority appear within the same **D**iscussion or section of the memo?
>
> **O:** does the previous citation refer to only **O**ne source? Id. should not be used if the immediately preceding citation is a string citation with more than one source because the reader would not know to which source the id. citation was referring.
>
> **E:** will the reader be able to locate the full citation with **E**ase?

If you are citing to the same source as in the previous citation but to a different location within that source, you must indicate the change in location with a page or section number after id. However, be careful with this, because there is a different format for documents with section or paragraph numbers (statutes, court transcripts, motions, etc.) and for sources with page numbers (cases, journal articles, etc.). The former, section and paragraph id. citations, do not include the word "at." For example:

- 28 U.S.C. § 53(c) (2006).
  Id. § 53(d).
- Gideon v. Wainwright, 372 U.S. 335, 340 (1963).
  Id. at 336.

String Citations: How to Cite to More Than One Authority

String citations are citation sentences that contain multiple authorities. For example, when a rule of law you have just stated appears in multiple sources, and you need your reader to know that, you might use a string cite. To cite authorities in a string citation you use the same rules as in a singular citation sentence. You can short cite within a string citation and you can use id., provided that the immediately preceding citation is not also a string cite and therefore contains more than one authority.

However, string citations follow a proper order which is found in Rule 1.4. Separate each authority with a semicolon (;) and in general, use the following order, but always check with the *Bluebook* if you use additional types of authorities in your citation.

- Statutes come before cases. Cite federal statutes before state statutes.
- Cases are cited:
  - Federal cases followed by state cases. Cite the cases from highest court to lowest, i.e. supreme court, appellate court, trial court.
  - If you cite more than one case from the same court, cite the cases in reverse chronological order, i.e. the most recent case first. Like this:
- N.M. Stat. Ann. § 30-2-1(A)(1) (West 2011); State v. Dowling, 257 P.3d 930, 934 (N.M. 2011); State v. Martinez, 45 P.3d 41, 42 (N.M. Ct. App. 2002); Henry v. State, 32 P.3d 38, 39 (N.M. Ct. App. 2001).

Constructing a Journal or Law Review Citation

To cite a journal article, follow Rule 16. Rule 16 also shows how to cite to other periodicals such as newspapers and magazines.

General format: Author (First name, Last name), *Title of Article*, V <Journ. Abbrev.= Pa, Pi (date).

- V is the Volume of the journal where the article is found.
- Pa is the first page on which the article appears in the volume.
- Pi is the pincite for the information you are citing from the article.

Style of Journal Citations:

- The author of the article should appear in Regular Roman Font.
- The title of the article should be underlined in memos and briefs, and italicized in journal articles and footnotes.
- The abbreviation for the journal in which the article appears should be in regular roman font in memos and briefs, and in large and small caps in journal articles and footnotes.
- Do not put the author's last name first; begin the citation with the author's name as it appears on the title page of the article.
- If there is more than one author, use the ampersand (&) and commas to separate the authors, like so:

- Frederico Cheever, Julianna Terrazas & Jane B. Spence.
- In order to abbreviate the journal in which the article appears, look up the journal's name in Table T13.
  - T13 includes the major legal journals and others that frequently appear in legal writing. If you are citing an article from a journal that is not listed in the table, look up each word of the journal's title in T13 and any geographical term in T10 and use those abbreviations.

Example:

- Laura Kalman, Border Patrol: Reflections on the Turn to History in Legal Scholarship, 68 Fordham L. Rev. 87, 90–91 (1997).

Formula for Creating a Citation to the Internet

Rule 18 governs Internet and other electronic sources. This is the part of the *Bluebook* that has seen the most changes in the past few years and will doubtless see more in the future as additional electronic platforms and resources become acceptable for citation in the legal profession.

Read Rule 18 carefully as the citations for different types of Internet sources are different. Because this rule varies so much, only the citation most likely to appear in first year assignments is discussed below.

In general, citations to the Internet are used only when a print source is not available. However, with the increasing availability of useful legal documents on the Web, the *Bluebook* R18.2.2 recommends including a parallel citation to the Internet when the URL will "substantially improve access to the source cited." The citation format for the parallel citation is

- <Citation of print source=, available at http://www.<URL>.

  For example:

  - Denver, Colo., Mun. Code. tit. II ch. 5–13 (2009), available at http://library.municode.com/index.aspx?clientId=1025.
  - Letter from Deval L. Patrick, Assistant Att'y Gen., Civil Rights Div., to Sen. Tom Harkin (Sept. 9, 1996), available at http://www.justice.gov/crt/foia/cltr204.txt.
- Note regarding computer software: To make your legal documents appear as professional as possible, remove the automatic correction that creates hyperlinks for web addresses in your word processor. In Microsoft Word, right click on the hyperlink and click *edit hyperlink*, then *remove hyperlink*. At that time the option should be available to turn off automatic creation of hyperlinks.

Introductory Signals, B1.2 and R1.2

Legal writers use introductory signals to citations as a simple way to inform the reader about how the citation relates to the information provided in the text. Signals are capitalized when they begin a citation sentence and lower case when they are used to begin a subsequent citation clause. In court documents and memoranda, signals are underlined separately from the case name. In journal articles and books, signals are in italics.

- **No signal:** Do not include a signal with your citation when: (1) you are citing an authority that directly states the proposition; (2) you are citing the source of a quotation; or (3) you are citing an authority referred to in the preceding text.
- **See:** Use see to cite to an authority that does not directly state but clearly supports your proposition.
- **E.g.,:** Use e.g., to cite to an authority that is one of multiple authorities or jurisdictions directly stating the same proposition.
- **But see:** Use but see when citing authority that is contrary to your proposition.

Carefully look at Rules 1.2 and 1.3 for additional signals and how to order signals should you need to use multiple signals within the same citation. For example:

- See Carparts Distribution Ctr., Inc. v. Auto. Wholesaler's Ass'n of New Eng., Inc., 37 F.3d 12, 19 (1st Cir. 1994).
- Id.; see, e.g., Stoutenborough v. Nat'l Football League, (establishing that the ADA covers "all of the services which the public accommodation offers").
- See Doe v. Mut. of Omaha Ins. Co., 179 F.3d 557, 559 (7th Cir. 1999) (in dicta). But see Parker v. Metro. Life Ins. Co., 121 F.3d 1006, 1014 (6th Cir. 1997) (holding public accommodations are only physical places).

Parenthetical Information, Rule 1.5

As in two of the above examples, sometimes you will want to include a parenthetical at the end of your citation to explain the relevance of what you are citing to your proposition. When using the signals see also, cf., compare ... with..., but cf., and see generally, it is strongly recommended that you include a parenthetical explaining the reason for including the citation. There are three main types of parentheticals: explanatory, descriptive, and quotation.

Explanatory parentheticals do not begin with a capital letter and usually begin with a word ending in "ing." For example:

- See also Parker v. Metro. Life Ins. Co., 121 F.3d 1006, 1014 (6th Cir. 1997) (holding public accommodations are only physical places).

Quotation parentheticals should quote one or more full sentence (or a portion of the material that represents a full sentence) and begin with a capital letter and end with appropriate punctuation. For example:

- Rubio v. State, 194 P.3d 1224, 1229 (2008) ("A defendant is entitled to effective assistance of counsel, as guaranteed by the Sixth Amendment of the United States Constitution, when deciding whether to accept or reject a plea bargain.").

Citing to Court Documents, B.17

With brief writing, you will be required to cite the facts of your case to the record or to other court documents filed in your case. This helps a judge to locate any disputed facts among the parties. A citation to a court name includes: (1) the abbreviated name of the document; (2) a pinpoint citation; and (3) the date of the document if necessary. The court document citation follows your textual citation, and may or may not be enclosed in parentheses.

The Name of the Document

The name of the document should be abbreviated according to Bluepages table B.T1. For example, when citing to the Record of the case, abbreviate to R. When citing to an Attorney Affidavit, abbreviate to Att'y Aff.

Pinpoint Citations

With court documents, pincites should be as precise as possible. For example, cite to the page and paragraph or line number on which the material appears. Page numbers do not need to be identified by "p." but other subdivisions should be identified (*e.g.*, ¶). For most court documents you do not need to introduce a pincite with "at." The exception is that a reference to the case record does include "at." For example: R. at 86.

Date

The date of the court document should be included in your citation when: (1) two or more documents have the same name; (2) the date of the document is significant to your argument; or (3) to avoid confusion.

Examples of Record Citations

- Jerry Canato, a blind musician, uses the convenience of the internet to safely access the community and purchase goods from within his own home. Compl. ¶¶ 1, 7.
- Smith admitted he did not return home the day of the attack until after it was dark. Smith Aff. 3, May 9, 2011.

Citing to Quotations, Rule 5

When a quotation within the text of a legal document is over 50 words, the quote should appear as a block quote. That is, it should be indented on the left and right without any quotation marks. The source of the block quotation should follow on the next line and should not be indented with the block quote. When the quote is less than 50 words the quote should exist within the normal text enclosed within quotation marks. With legal documents, the citation should immediately follow the quote. Where the beginning of the quoted sentence is being omitted, capitalize the first letter of the quoted language and place it in brackets if it is not already capitalized. Where the end of a quoted sentence is being omitted, insert an ellipsis between the last word being quoted and the final punctuation of the sentence being quoted. For example:

> "[C]urriculum was usually rudimentary ... the school term was but three months a year in many states. . . ." Brown v. Bd. of Educ. of Topeka, 347 U.S. 483, 490 (1954).

Practice Exercise 1: When to Cite

Review the excerpts below and choose whether to cite or leave the excerpt without a cite:

- The *Goller* court retained two exceptions under which children still would not be allowed to bring tort actions against their parents: "(1) where the alleged negligent act involves an exercise of parental authority over the child and (2) where the alleged negligent act involves an exercise of ordinary parental discretion with respect to the provision of food, clothing, housing, medical and dental services, and other care."
- *The following appears immediately after the information (and a proper cite) in the previous question:* "The second exception concerns matters involving an exercise of parental discretion."
- Employers must have taken measures to prevent the secret from becoming available to a person other than one selected by the owner and such precautions must be more than normal business procedures.

Practice Exercise 2: Using the Index

Try to find the relevant rule on how to cite the following less frequently cited sources.

- A letter
- The Bible
- A congressional hearing
- A Canadian Supreme Court case

(*Answers on the following page.*)

Practice Exercise Answers

Exercise 1:

- Cite. Here, the author used a direct quote of the holding/rule of a case and therefore a citation is absolutely required.
- No cite. The author here was simply making an additional statement about what an exception covers, so it is assumed that it appears in the same location as the previous citation.
- Cite. This is a synthesized rule and the author would want to cite here because it would lend authority to her rule and also allow a judge or senior attorney to read the sources that led to the creation of the rule.

Exercise 2:

- Rule 17.2.3
- Rule 15.8(c)
- Rule 13.3
- T2.6

Further Reading

Tracy L. McGaugh & Christine Hurt, *Interactive Citation Workbook for The Bluebook: A Uniform System of Citation* (LexisNexis, 2012).

Linda J. Barris, *Understanding and Mastering The Bluebook* (Carolina Academic Press, 2010).

Exercise

Review additional exercises online. Then take the quiz (also online), and then complete the citation modules as they are assigned by your professor.

As You Prepare These Assignments, Consider the Following

Are you beginning to understand the purpose of legal citations?

Are you beginning to understand the overall structure of citations and how they generally work?

Are you gradually getting more comfortable with the *Bluebook*?

Have you added reference tabs to your *Bluebook*? Did it help?

ONLINE: Citation quiz, links to the Lexis ICW Exercises, and the Bluebook tabbing guide.

Chapter 8

Writing Well

Introduction

Your reader should not have to read a sentence twice because it does not make sense the first time. If a reader thinks a sentence is unclear, it probably is. This chapter focuses on making your sentences clear, on using an effective legal writing style, on learning the mechanics of legal writing, and on understanding the steps in the legal writing process.

Knowing Your Audience

Before you begin to plan a piece of legal writing it is critical to understand who your audience will be. Lawyers write for many different audiences, including clients, judges, and other lawyers. You should always be conscious of who you are writing for and adjust your tone and level of discourse accordingly. Writing for your senior attorney is quite different from writing a brief for a trial or an appellate court judge. When writing a memorandum, your senior attorney will be looking for objective writing that explains what the law is and how it applies to the senior attorney's current case. In a memorandum, the writer should not be advocating for the client but rather explaining how the law applies to the client's case. In contrast, a brief for a trial or appellate court should persuade the reader, a judge, why your argument is the best interpretation and embodiment of the law, so brief writing should be persuasive.

Clarity and Conciseness

> "The most valuable of all talents is that of never using two words when one will do." — Thomas Jefferson

Legal writing should be clear and concise because those who will read your writing — other lawyers, judges, and clients — are busy, and they expect to understand what you have written on the first time through. The following are some techniques to keep in mind when crafting clear and cogent prose.

First, using Richard Wydick's concept of "working words" versus "glue words"[11] is a great way to identify problematic or verbose sentences. Working words carry the

11. Richard C. Wydick, *Plain English for Lawyers* 9–12 (5th ed. 2005).

meaning of the sentence while the glue words hold the sentence together grammatically. To be coherent every sentence must have both types of words, but too many glue words will lead to a poorly constructed sentence, so you want to have as few glue words as possible. Consider the following examples:

A trial by jury was requested by the defendant.

- Working words: trial, jury, requested, defendant (4 out of 9).
- Glue words: A, by, was, by, the (5 out of 9).

The defendant requested a jury trial.

- Working words: defendant, requested, jury, trial (4 out of 6).
- Glue words: the, a (2 out of 6).[12]

As you can see, not only is the second sentence shorter, it is also more direct and uses fewer glue words. Using fewer glue words generally leads to better sentence flow and a more easily understood sentence. While this technique is helpful to identify excess words in your sentences, sometimes the best thing is to just write plainly and simply in the first instance, with one or two concepts in each sentence. Here is an example from a typical first year law student's mid-semester memo:

> In the present case, Mr. Locust himself did not communicate to his psychiatrist specific and detailed threats regarding Ms. Keene, although Mr. Locust did have a history of violence against those who had wronged him.

While that sentence communicates helpful information, it could have accomplished the same in fewer words. Like this:

> Here, Locust did not communicate specific threats to his psychiatrist, but he did have a history of violence.

Second, in addition to removing excess words and writing simply, you want to use the active voice in your legal writing as much as possible. Active voice means that the subject of the sentence performs the action expressed by the verb. "Joe kicked the football downfield." In passive voice, the subject of the sentence receives the action expressed by the verb. "The ball was kicked downfield by Joe."

You have heard this before from teachers you have had in school or in college, but it is especially important for legal writing. Too much passive voice in your writing will confuse the reader and they will lose the point of what you are trying to communicate. Also, if the author overuses passive voice, the reader will lose interest. You do not want a judge or senior partner to become bored in your work and stop reading. Also, in legal memos and briefs you will often be explaining complex legal issues. Writing active and concise sentences will make your points easier to understand.

---

12. *Id.* at 10.

Third, although the temptation will be great, avoid quoting large portions of text from a statute or a case in your legal writing. Instead, quote only key terms or language that you want to highlight for your reader, and which you are about to explain or address in greater detail. You provide value to your reader when you do the work of interpreting what you read, rather than ask you reader to read it too. Another advantage of selecting the key terms and quoting just that much is that by doing so you highlight for your reader that those terms are important.

Fourth, you want to avoid in your legal writing the use of "throat clearing" or "filler phrases," such as "it is generally recognized that...," "it is understood that...," "it should be noted that...," and "it is important to note that..." Just get right to the point instead of using phrases like these. If the principle you are explaining is *not* generally recognized, understood, or important to note, there would be little reason to include it in the document you are writing.

On the other hand, words that *are* useful in legal writing are words that transition between one point and another, and show a relationship between those points. Transition words or phrases such as "in contrast," "accordingly," "because," "thus," and "therefore" help the reader follow where you are headed in your analysis. Transition words also specify the relationship between ideas and help set apart and identify the author's important points and conclusions.[13]

Another aid to clarity in legal writing is to write in the affirmative, not the negative. Writing in the affirmative is more declarative, while writing in the negative forces the reader to spend time and intellectual energy figuring out the opposite of what you wrote. Writing in the affirmative makes ideas and sentences more straightforward and easier to understand. For example:

> Like the website in the Access Now case, the Jeff's List website exists solely in cyberspace and lacks a physical structure.

Punctuation and Grammar

The level of discourse in the law is sophisticated enough that you are expected to know the basics of grammar and punctuation. If you did not have these drilled into your head in your previous schooling, you will need to study them and make your best effort to master them now. These basics are expected by your audience (other lawyers and judges) because in the law, grammar and punctuation can be incredibly important. For example, in contract disputes, the placement of a comma can become the basis of a ruling and cause parties to hire "grammar experts" on appeal.[14] Trial

---

13. There is an excellent list of transitions used in legal writing that you can find in Anne Enquist & Laurel Currie Oates, *Just Writing: Grammar, Punctuation, and Style for the Legal Writer* 56–57 (5th ed. 2017).

14. *See* Ian Austen, *The Comma that Costs One Million Dollars (Canadian)*, N.Y. Times p. A1 (Oct. 25, 2006), *available at* http://www.nytimes.com/2006/10/25/business/worldbusiness/25comma.html#.

and appellate judges have admonished lawyers for poor grammar in their opinions.[15] Here are some of the common grammatical errors that writers make.[16]

1. *Who vs. Whom*: The best way to determine which pronoun to use is to delete the subject/verb immediately after the "who" or "whom." If the sentence still makes sense use "who"; if it does not make sense use "whom." For example:

   Incorrect: Officer Johnson questions the man whom ~~he thought~~ witnessed the robbery.

   Correct: Officer Johnson questioned the man who ~~he thought~~ witnessed the robbery.

2. *Affect vs. Effect: Affect* is used as a verb meaning to influence, impress, or sway, or as a verb meaning to pretend or feign. For example:

   The Appellate Court did not seem to be affected by the policy argument in the brief.

   Effect is most commonly used as a noun meaning result, consequence or outcome. Effect can also be a verb meaning to bring about or accomplish. For example:

   The guardian ad litem successfully effected a parenting plan that was in the best interests of his clients, the children of the marriage.

   If "affect" were used in the above sentence, the meaning would have been that the guardian ad litem influenced the parenting plan as opposed to reaching an agreed upon parenting plan. (Note: the grammar check feature on most word processors will tell you that "effected" should be changed to "affected" in the above sentence because influenced is the more common meaning, so do not rely on your grammar checking software in legal writing.)

3. *Then vs. Than:* Use "than" for comparisons such as "worse than," "higher than," "less than," etc. Use "then" for time: "I saw a man run from the building right before it caught fire, and then I called the police."

4. *Court:* Court is a collective noun and should be paired with the singular pronoun "it." Never refer to a court as "they." The word "court" should be capitalized in only the following instances:

---

15. *See* Robin Mashal, *Federal Judge Admonishes Lawyer for Grammatical and Typographical Errors*, http://www.lawlink.com/documents/2896/public (last visited June 3, 2017). The Judge's order finds that the Plaintiff's motion is denied "without prejudice for … otherwise being riddled with grammatical and typographical errors that nearly render the entire motion incomprehensible." The Judge also orders that the offending lawyer reread the Local and Federal Rules of Civil Procedure and hand-deliver a copy of the order to his client no later than 6 days after the date of the order with a certificate compliance to be filed with the court.

16. Portions of this section owe a debt to the legal writing style book, Anne Enquist & Laurel Currie Oates, *Just Writing: Grammar, Punctuation, and Style for the Legal Writer* 231–35, 317–23 (5th ed. 2017). This excellent book (or a similar legal writing style manual) is a recommended companion to this text, since this section only addresses a few highlights of common problems found in legal writing. There are many more, and the Enquist & Oates text addresses them with great care and detail.

a. When referring to a Court in full:

The United States Court of Appeals for the Tenth Circuit is based in Denver, Colorado.

b. When referring to the United States Supreme Court:

Justice Marshall wrote the unanimous opinion of the Court.

c. When referring to the court that will be receiving your document:

The Court should deny the Defendant's motion to dismiss.

In all other instances, "court" should be lower case. For example:

The Miller court considered only the first two factors.

The court in the Ronald case found the defendant did not have a reasonable belief of imminent death or great bodily harm.

5. *No "I" in Legal Writing:* Avoid first and second person references in your legal writing. The use of "I" and "you" makes the writing less formal and sound is as if the lawyer is speaking to the court or senior attorney as a friend or in a colloquial setting; this is inappropriate for memos and briefs.
6. *Semicolons vs. Colons:* Semicolons are generally used to separate main clauses not joined by a coordinating conjunction such as "and," and to separate items in a series if the list is long or if one or more of the items has internal commas. Colons are most often used to introduce a list of items or quotations. For example:

The Plaintiff here has sustained significant damages: a broken jaw that cannot be completely repaired, leading to permanent disfigurement; speech impediments; pain and suffering; and loss of future wages as a syndicated radio show host.

Writing Preparation

Excellent legal writing certainly benefits from understanding these rules and preferences. But the best legal writing often comes after you have taken considerable time to plan and organize your ideas before you even start to write. Depending on your learning style and preferences, this preparation can take many forms. The organizational scheme that works best for you is the one you should use, but keep in mind that you may only settle on it after many writing assignments and through attempting several different methods. Described here are two of the most common methods of planning out your writing; they can be used together or separately. Examples of both methods can also be found in the online supplement.

The Thick Outline

The "thick" outline is more than your standard outline. A thick outline may begin with the standard Roman numeral organization with key phrases and topics, but when "thickened" evolves into a much more user friendly and helpful document to support the writing phase. With a thick outline you begin with key phrases and topics, but then you go back and fill in the key *phrases and topics* with key *law and facts* from cases, *useful quotes*, and *holdings*, and the outline becomes thicker. Thick outlines should also include your overview and thesis paragraphs (see Chapter 6) so that you can begin to see your theory of the case develop and address any gaps or problematic organizational issues. If your word processor has a comment function, you could use it to make notes to yourself in the margins about issues that are still problematic or under consideration. Consider the following example of a thick outline for a two-issue brief:

I. The ADA applies to online auction websites because the plain language of the statute includes virtual spaces and the website has a nexus with a physical place of public accommodation.

- Overview: Title III of the ADA prohibits discrimination against the disabled in places of public accommodation that effect commerce. Americans with Disabilities Act of 1990, 42 U.S.C § 12181 (2009). A place of public accommodation is defined in a twelve-part categorized list that includes sales and rental establishments and places of public display or collection. Id. § 12181(7)(A–H). Discrimination occurs by denial of the full and equal enjoyment of the goods, services, and activities of any place of public accommodation. Id. § 12182(a). The *Federal Register* defines "full and equal enjoyment" as the right to participate and to have an equal opportunity to obtain the same results as others to the extent possible with such accommodations. Nondiscrimination on the Basis of Disability by Public Accommodations and in Commercial Facilities, 28 C.F.R. pt. 36.201.
- The defendant discriminated against Mr. Canato and other similarly situated visually impaired Internet users by not making his auction website compatible with most popular screen reader software. (Compl. ¶ 19.) The defendant states in his motion to dismiss that Mr. Canato has failed to state a claim because his company, Jim's List, is not a place of public accommodation covered by Title III of the ADA. (Mot. To Dismiss ¶ I.) However, Jim's List is a place of public accommodation under Title III because precedent suggests that the plain language of the public accommodation statute is not limited to bricks and mortar physical locations; and even if the language is construed narrowly to apply only to physical locations, Jim's List has a nexus with a physical place of public accommodation and thus falls under the auspices of Title III. Precedent regarding the interpretation of the statute and the nexus test make Mr. Canato's claim inappropriate for dismissal.

II. Virtual businesses are public accommodations because the language of the statute includes broad terms applicable to such businesses and encompasses intangible barriers.

- Thesis: Include tangible/intangible analysis (Rendon v. Valley Crest Prods., Ltd., 294 F.3d 1279 (11th Cir. 2002)), travel service analysis (Carparts Distrib. Ctr., Inc. v. Auto. Wholesaler's Ass'n of New England, Inc., 37 F. 3d 12 (1st Cir. 1994)/ Doe v. Mut. of Omaha Ins. Co., 179 F.3d 557 (7th Cir. 1999)) and place of sale being irrelevant (Morgan v. Joint Admin. Bd., Ret. Plan of The Pillsbury Co., 268 F.3d 456 (7th Cir. 2001)).

- Travel Service Analysis/place of sale irrelevant

  i. Carparts: at 19. Plain meaning of § 12181(7) does not require places of public accommodation to have physical structures for person to enter. Public accommodation is ambiguous at best and agency regulations and public policy concerns persuades the court that the phrase is not limited to actual physical structures. Use travel services as an example—Congress clearly contemplated that service establishments include providers of services which do not require a person to physically enter a physical structure.

MindMapping

Another method of organizing legal writing is "mapping" your organizational scheme as you develop it. This method is ideal for visual learners and those who need to "see" their organizational scheme develop. Programs such as Mindjet's MindManager (www.mindjet.com) and Scapple (www.literatureandlatte.com) provide easy ways for you to map your thinking on a particular legal issue. Both programs are available for download on free 30-day trials. For a lower-tech option, you could also map your issues on a large easel-sized Post-It pad. A finished mapping project can look like a brainstorming wheel. An example that shows the mapping of a legal document is provided online.

Further Reading

Anne Enquist & Laurel Currie Oates, *Just Writing: Grammar, Punctuation, and Style for the Legal Writer* (4th ed. 2013).

Richard C. Wydick, *Plain English for Lawyers* (5th ed., Carolina Academic Press, 2005).

Exercise

Editing exercise: Find a poorly drafted memo and edit it, looking for proofreading mistakes as well as citation errors. Also, explore a paper-based approach to MindMapping, or download a free trial of either MindManager (PC) or Scapple (Mac) (or similar software) to test out the process of visualizing the development of your legal argument.

As You Prepare This Assignment, Consider the Following

As you work on the editing exercise, does it remind you of mistakes that you often make?

Make a list of those mistakes you commonly make, and consider how you might avoid making such mistakes in the future.

As you try "thick" outlining, and test out Mindmapping software, how is it working for you? Do you have a preference of one method over the other?

ONLINE: Editing exercise, links to MindMapping software, and an example of a thick outline in a MindMap form.

Chapter 9

Editing and Proofreading

"The essence of writing is rewriting."[17]

Introduction

At least three things are starkly different about legal writing from other types of composition. First, as you have probably gathered by now, lawyers write a lot. And their writing matters. It matters to the efficient functioning of their law office, it matters to their clients, and it matters to the courts. Second, legal writing does not flow freely the first time you sit down to write. Good legal writing requires a lot more time spent in the preparatory "thinking and linking" phase than most other forms of writing. You have to have a very good idea of what you want to say before you start. Third, even if you do have a good idea of what you want and need to say, it does not always come out the most effective way the first time. The topics legal writing addresses are often complicated, and explaining something complicated is difficult. Making them luminously clear and easy to understand is still more difficult. Achieving clarity often takes careful revision. Good lawyers are not just good writers but excellent editors of their own work as well.

The work product of lawyers is expected to be clean and free of errors. As noted in the chapter on citation, judges and colleagues consider sloppy cites to reflect poorly on the attorney who submitted the document. The same is true of a document that is poorly edited, not correctly formatted, or that has typographical errors. Many judges have publicly chastised lawyers for submitting documents that contain numerous errors and typos. You do not want to be one of those lawyers, so learning to proofread your own work with care and precision is an additional lawyering skill you need to develop.

A well-constructed document that is free of errors supports more than your credibility and reputation. It also makes the document more authoritative and trustworthy. Even one poorly constructed sentence or a simple typo can undermine that effect. So it is important to rid your work of confusing sentences and take the time to polish the final product. If you do, it will advance the persuasive strength of your work.

Editing is not the same thing as proofreading. When you edit your work, you are seeking to improve your organization, clarity, and precision. When you proofread,

17. William Zinsser, *On Writing Well* (2009).

you are looking for smaller mistakes, such as missing words, typos, misspellings, and incorrect punctuation.

Editing

Professional writers often speak of putting their drafts in the "top drawer"—putting it out of sight for a while—so they can return to it with fresh eyes. You should do the same. Coming back to your work after some rest and time spent on other projects will allow you to look at it more objectively. Print out a fresh copy and try to put yourself in your reader's position, reading it as they would. Focus first on the "large-scale" organization of the document, assessing the clarity and strength of its overall structure. Should one issue come before the other for clarity, or should one sub-section come before the one you have in the draft now? Also consider content. Are all aspects of the issue included or is there a missing element in your analysis? Consider whether all elements you have included are really needed. You do not want to include a section or sub-section that has little bearing on the conclusion (or result) of the analysis you are offering the reader. If it is superfluous, remove it.

Having edited the document's overall structure, turn next to the paragraph level. Does each paragraph contain all it should to advance the analysis? If you need an additional case to flesh out one of your rule explanations, return to your research, select it, and add it in. Or, are there two very similar cases, only one of which you need? If so, select the weaker one and remove it. To select the weaker one, look for the case that (for example) is not in your jurisdiction or for which the facts and holding are less applicable to the client's case than the other cases you are citing.

Then turn to the sentence level for a close edit. Take out any extra words. Try to say it plainly rather than dress it up with extra verbiage. Legal writing puts a premium on being clear and plainly stated. Is each sentence clear and direct? If not, pretend you are explaining the matter to a young child. This may force you to make it simple and straightforward.

Finally, read the document out loud. A stumble or long pause as you read probably means that your reader would also stumble or pause at that spot. Mark it for a further edit. Reading out loud also will help you determine whether or not the sentences and paragraphs flow well, and whether your transitions between paragraphs are working.

While it is important to edit your work carefully, you do not want to overdo it and not leave enough time for the next stage: proofreading.

Proofreading

It is vital to save time before a deadline to proofread your document because it should be done carefully, slowly, with a clear head, and ideally in a quiet room. As with editing, it is a good idea to take a break before you start so you will have perspective on your work. This means that, with the need for both editing and proofreading stages, you should plan to start your writing earlier than you may have been used to in the past. Legal writing takes large amounts of thought, care, and precision.

The hardest thing about proofreading your own work is that you know what you meant to write even if your fingers did not actually write what you intended. An example is shown in this well-known excerpt:

> Aoccdrnig to rscheearch at an Elingsh uinervtisy, it deosn't mttaer in waht oredr the ltteers in a wrod are, olny taht the frist and lsat ltteres are at the rghit pcleas.

Creepy, huh? But to be a good proofreader of your own work, you have to develop strategies to combat this tendency. Here are some methods you might try:

- Read your document with a cover sheet. Reading with a cover sheet forces you to proofread line-by-line. Seeing fewer words as you pass down the page makes it easier to catch spelling and typographical errors.
- Do not rely on spell checking software embedded in your word processing software. Remember, word processors do not catch when a writer uses the wrong word (i.e., their, there, or they're).
- As you get more practice with proofreading, it will help to gather a list of the types of errors you commonly make. You may have trouble with apostrophes, for example. Or distinguishing the difference between "Its" and "It's." Once you know your common problems, read your document looking specifically for those sorts of mistakes.
- It is a good idea to print out a copy of your document. It is easier, at least for most people, to see mistakes on a printed page than on a screen.
- Read the document with a pencil pointing to each word. By pointing at each word you will see just that word. This will increase your ability to catch spelling and typographical errors.
- Highlight each citation in your document and check each separately, both for correct form and for typos.

Further Reading

William K. Zinsser, *On Writing Well* (6th ed., Harper Reference, 1998).

Anne Enquist & Laurel Currie Oates, *Just Writing: Grammar, Punctuation, and Style for the Legal Writer* (5th ed. Wolters Kluwer, 2017).

Exercise

Complete the Editing and Proofreading Assignment posted online. Conduct a separate editing phase and a proofreading phase on one of the major documents you are producing in your class.

As You Prepare This Assignment, Consider the Following

Did you read your draft out loud?

Did you find any structural problems in your document?

Did you find any clotted or complex sentences in your writing, and were you able to fix them?

Did it work to simply split a too long or too complex sentence into two sentences?

Which editing and proofreading techniques work best for you?

ONLINE: Editing and Proofreading Assignment, and an Editing Checklist.

Chapter 10

Contract Drafting

Introduction

Knowing how to draft a contract is an important skill for every lawyer to have, even if you will not be a transactional lawyer. Contract drafting is a vital function of many law firms and corporations and you may commonly find yourself reviewing a contract even if you specialize in litigation. Like any legal writing, good contract drafting requires knowing applicable law, critically evaluating available information, knowing who the audience is, and writing in a clear and organized manner. However, drafting contracts is different from most legal writing because the goal is not to explain a legal analysis or to persuade someone of a position, but rather to clearly detail an agreement between parties in a way that minimizes risk and provides for remedies in the future.

Purpose of a Contract

The purpose of a contract is to accurately embody all the negotiated terms between the parties to the contract. While drafting the contract, you should consider the Three "Ps": (1) Predict, (2) Provide, and (3) Protect. You must **Predict** what may happen between the parties, **Provide** for that contingency in the contract, and **Protect** your client's interests with a remedy in the event of a breach. When drafting a contract, you will want to accomplish the Three Ps efficiently and effectively by using language that is clear, concise, and well organized. A third-party reader should be able to read the contract and understand all the terms even though they were not involved in the negotiation or the drafting of the contract.

Language of Drafting

A great deal of litigation arises out of poor drafting of contracts. Drafting efficiently and effectively depends on both the substance of the contract and the style of the drafting. Stylistically, a contract should be written in plain language and should be free of superfluous words so a reader can easily understand the provisions. A contract should also be written in the present tense even though it provides for actions that may arise in the future. Present tense is preferable because the contract, when read, applies to the current situation. When drafting contracts, you should also use the active voice. Active sentences must have actors while passive sentences can be complete without them, so using active voice helps minimize any confusion about which party is the responsible actor for which provisions. Pronouns should rarely be used in the contract; they can create confusion as to which party is being addressed. Instead, use gender-neutral language. A contract is on-going and may be assigned to another party; a contract should apply to whoever may become a party to it. You can refer to the parties by their names, but better practice is to refer to them by their legal label, such as grantor/grantee or lessor/lessee.

When drafting a contract, you will be creating provisions for obligations, conditions, and authorizations. To create these provisions, and to avoid confusion, you will have to be especially careful about the language you use. For example, in the English language the word "shall" has several different meanings. "Shall" can refer to a requirement or to something in the future. The drafter should use specific language to convey specific contractual rights and requirements. When drafting contracts the following terms should be used with these meanings:

- ***Shall*—Obligations (a required action that if not performed is a breach of contract)**

  Florist shall make initial delivery to Client 30 days after order.

- ***Shall not*—Prohibitions (an action that is specifically disallowed)**

  Client shall not order flowers or plants from any other florist.

- ***May*—Authorization (a privilege, but not a duty)**

  Client may order more plants or flowers at any time during Agreement term.

- ***Must*—Conditions (a contingency, but not a promise to perform)**

  Client must return all vases to Florist at the termination of Agreement or else Florist will charge Client $25 fee for each vase not returned.

You will want to be consistent with the language used and need to make sure to correctly identify whether the client wants to create an obligation, authorization, or a condition.

Structure of a Contract

Heading

The heading of a contract is also referred to as a "title." The heading should describe the contract. The heading should not be too general or too specific, but rather written to effectively and efficiently let a reader know what the contract is about. A contract can be called a "contract" or an "agreement," but the drafter should be consistent in whichever term is used.

Example:

Floral Service Agreement

Caption

The caption goes directly below the heading and is an introduction to the document. Although this is the first paragraph of the contract, it is not a numbered section. In this section the drafter should name the parties, explain the nature of the agreement, and detail any important dates. The drafter should use the full, correct name of the parties, but a "shorthand name" may be given to the parties in this section to use throughout the rest of the document (ex: John Smith ("Lessee")). When describing the nature of the agreement, the drafter should provide a more detailed explanation of what is in the Heading. The date of the contract can reflect the effective date, the signed date, or the date performance begins, so it is essential to expressly identify which date is being used.

Example:

> This is a Floral Service Agreement ("Agreement") entered into August 1, 2017, between Flowers by Yvonne, 311 Tulip Avenue, Whitman, NY ("Florist"), and Sterling Cooper, Inc., 251 Madison Avenue, Whitman, NY ("Client").

Recitals

Recitals describe the background, assumptions, and intentions of the contract. The recitals should not include any substantive provisions. This section is usually written as statements of "whereas" with a conclusion of "therefore." Recitals are not necessary for every contract and are often misused. You will need to be careful in correctly and effectively using recitals when drafting a contract.

Example:

> WHEREAS Client would like to enhance Client's company image by decorating the main lobby and reception areas on the three floors of the Client's corporate offices with flowers and live plants; and
>
> WHEREAS Florist provides live flowers and plants as well as floral servicing for corporate offices.
>
> THEREFORE parties agree to enter this Agreement for the floral servicing of Client's corporate headquarters as follows:

Definitions

Definitions are used to avoid ambiguity and ambivalence within a contract. It is important to remember that using definitions can make a word inclusive or exclusive of other meaning; a list of specifics is treated as exhaustive. Definitions eliminate the need to repeatedly use long definitions within the terms. Definitions should be unnumbered paragraphs and be listed in alphabetical order. Definitions, like recitals, are not necessary for every contract and should only be used when appropriate. If you decide that definitions are not appropriate at the beginning of the contract, they can still be used within the contract, in this way: (Manufacturer shall deliver merchandise ("initial delivery") to retailer by October 22).

Example:

> **Appropriate and seasonal** means fresh flowers that are readily available and grown in the area.
>
> **Flowers** include any flowers that are un-potted and cut from their roots and placed in a floral arrangement.
>
> **Initial Delivery** means the first delivery of plants and first set of flowers.
>
> **Plants** include potted flowers, small plants, and small trees.
>
> **Service** means changing of flowers, watering plants, pruning plants (if needed), and removing dead leaves on or around plants.

Operative Language

The operative language of the contract is outlined by numbered paragraphs and describes the terms or substance of the contract. The terms are structured by topic and are preceded by an appropriate topic heading. The topics should be listed in a logical organization. Further, so as to give guidance to those reading or interpreting the contract, rules should be listed before exceptions and general terms should be listed before specific terms. That is, you should provide the basic terms of the contract before allowing for further descriptions or exceptions.

Example:

1. *Length of Agreement*

   Florist shall make initial delivery to Client 30 days after order is made. Florist shall start servicing plants and changing flowers the Monday following the initial delivery. This Agreement will be in effect for one year from initial delivery date.

2. *Flowers*

   Florist shall advise Client of which flowers are appropriate and seasonal. Client, however, shall make final decision on which flower arrangements are purchased for display. Florist shall change flowers at Client's office weekly. Client must notify Florist of the flower arrangements they want for the upcoming week at least 2 days before the delivery.

3. Plants

   Client shall choose plants from Florist's catalog at time of order. If Client requests a change of plants, Florist may charge Client $25 for delivery.

4. *Servicing*

   Florist shall service plants and flowers weekly. Florist shall service plants and flowers on Mondays. If a service day falls on a holiday or a day that Client's office is closed, Florist shall service plants and flowers the following day.

5. *Termination*

   Agreement automatically terminates at the end of one year from date of initial delivery. Client may renew Agreement for an additional year by notifying Florist, in writing, 30 days before the automatic termination of Agreement.

6. *Cancellation*

   Either party may cancel Agreement at any time with notice to the non-cancelling party. Cancelling party shall send a written notification of intent to cancel to non-cancelling party 30 days before requested cancellation date.

This section is also where you can add any boilerplate provisions that the parties feel are appropriate and necessary for the contract. Boilerplate provisions commonly describe the private law that will govern the contract.

Example:

- *Mediation Clause*

  If a dispute arises out of this Agreement, and if the dispute cannot be settled through negotiation, parties agree to try, in good faith, to settle the dispute by mediation before resorting to arbitration, litigation, or some other dispute resolution procedure.

Closing

The closing includes the signatures of the parties and the date. The underline of the signatures should include the full, correct names of the parties with no abbreviations. If a corporation is one of the parties, make sure that the corporation's name is used for the signature line. Make sure that the date used does not contradict anything else already written in the contract.

Example:

Parties have received, read, and understand this Agreement.

______________________	______________________
Client, Sterling Cooper, Inc.	Date
______________________	______________________
Florist, Flowers by Yvonne	Date

Contract Disputes

Two of the most common reasons for contract disputes are the failure to include all possible issues and outcomes in the contract, and ambiguity in the provisions that are included. Leaving key terms (e.g., price or delivery dates) open for later discussion could make the contract unenforceable if the two parties cannot come to agreement on them later. Likewise, not addressing all possibilities, even the unlikely ones, can lead to problems if those possibilities do occur.

Ambiguous language within a contract can frustrate the goal of drafting a clear and concise contract. Ambiguity is created when a word or provision can be interpreted in more than one way. This can cause issues if the parties to a contract are using conflicting interpretations of a word or provision that can alter the contract to the detriment of the other. To help clear up any ambiguities, you can use recitals at the beginning of the contract to state the parties' assumptions and intentions. However, because courts generally interpret ambiguous language against the party that drafted the contract, it is best to draft the contract in a way that accounts for, or preferably omits, ambiguities. There are three areas where ambiguity is most often a problem: (1) describing characteristics or categories, (2) using modifiers, and (3) using synonyms.

1. Describing Characteristics or Categories

Ambiguity often arises when it is unclear whether the drafter intended to indicate two types of categories or two characteristics of one category. For example, in the statement "Owner shall not use the property for farming and ranching" it is unclear whether the Lessee cannot use the property for two separate categories (use of farming or use of ranching) or for only one category with two characteristics (for use of both farming and ranching). To solve this problem, you need to rewrite the sentence in one of two ways to convey the intended meaning. First, by applying the action to each class separately:

Owner shall not use the property for farming and shall not use the property for ranching.

Or, by adding the word "both" to show the intention that both characteristics must apply:

Owner shall not use the property for both farming and ranching.

2. Modifiers

Ambiguity can also arise when it is unclear whether an adjective modifies one noun or a series of nouns. For example, in the statement "supplier shall provide red paint and brushes" it is unclear whether the "red" applies to the paint *and* the brushes or just the paint. If you intend for the modifier to apply only to one item, you could rearrange the sentence in one of two ways:

Supplier shall provide brushes and red paint.

Or, you can use tabulations within the terms section so as not to confuse modifiers:

Supplier shall provide:

- *Red paint; and*
- *Brushes*

If you intend for the modifier to apply to both items, then the sentence can be rewritten with the modifier before each term:

Supplier shall provide red paint and red brushes.

Or, you can use tabulations here as well, but put the modifier in the sentence rather than the tabulations:

Supplier shall provide red:

- *Paint; and*
- *Brushes*

3. Synonyms

The use of synonyms can also create ambiguity because it becomes unclear whether each term has a different meaning, or if they are being used interchangeably. For example, a drafter of a lease agreement might use the words transfer, sublease, or assign to convey the same meaning. The drafter may also, however, want these terms to have slightly different meanings. To solve this problem, the drafter of the lease should pick one word and stick with it throughout the contract. The drafter can also use definitions at the beginning of the contract to define a word to include all the other synonyms. If the words are to have a slightly different meaning, then the definitions can help in this respect as well.

Further Reading

Tina L. Stark, *Drafting Contracts: How and Why Lawyers Do What They Do* (2nd ed., Wolters Kluwer, 2013).

Exercise

Review the contract examples online and complete the ambiguity practice problems. In addition, your professor may assign additional contract drafting exercises.

As You Prepare This Assignment, Consider the Following

What are the key provisions of the example contract?

Are these provisions mandatory obligations or privileges granted to the parties? How do you know?

How are the parties referred to throughout the contract? Are the references consistent?

Does the contract use active voice? Plain language? Present tense?

What are the parts included in the contract? Is anything missing?

Does the contract use any ambiguous language? If so, how might this language be interpreted differently?

ONLINE: Examples of boilerplate language for a contract, example contracts, and the ambiguity practice problems.

Chapter 11

Legal Persuasion

"Rhetoric may be defined as the faculty of observing in any given case the available means of persuasion."[18]

Introduction

A fundamental role for attorneys is to represent their client's interests and persuade others of the rightness of their client's cause. Thus attorneys are advocates, and advocates must be persuasive. How have you been persuasive in the past? What methods have you used to convince others of the rightness of your arguments? Was it simply by having the stronger logical argument? Logic is certainly a method of persuasion we all use in arguments that we make, but it is not always enough. The question of how to go about being persuasive in the law is not a simple one, and not just limited to offering the soundest legal analysis. One method is as old as the Greek philosophers.

Aristotle's Modes of Persuasion

Aristotle, a student of Plato and one of the founding fathers of western philosophy, lived from 384 to 322 B.C. Among the many philosophical topics that Aristotle wrote about was the art of persuasion, and he constructed a three-part framework with which to examine and explain it. In Aristotle's framework, "of the modes of persuasion furnished by the spoken word there are three kinds...." and he described them as Ethos, Pathos, and Logos.

In basic terms, ethos is the appeal based on the character of the speaker or author. Pathos is an appeal to passion or emotion. Logos is the appeal to logic or reason. An effective legal advocacy document, such as a demand letter or a legal brief, should ideally contain all three types of argument, for if it does so, it will be more persuasive.

"First, persuasion is achieved by the speaker's personal character when the speech is so spoken as to make us think him credible."[19]

For a lawyer, ethos involves establishing credibility with the court and with colleagues and opposing counsel. One way to enhance your credibility is to show respect for opposing counsel, and to acknowledge where her arguments might have merit,

---

18. Aristotle, *Rhetoric*, Chapter 2.

19. *Id.*

or where the two of you do not disagree. Also, a lawyer's credibility comes from reputation in the profession for attention to important details such as meeting court deadlines, providing accurate descriptions of the law, providing correct and helpful citations, and using proper grammar with a lack of typographical errors. In short, you should strive to make your advocacy writing respectful to opposing counsel and indicative of the reputation as a lawyer that you want to have.

> *"Secondly, persuasion may come through the hearers, when the speech stirs their emotions."*[20]

Pathos refers to arguments that are designed to stir the emotions of your audience and make them care about your client. The use of storytelling, themes, and literary devices in legal writing, which is discussed below, is within Aristotle's conception of Pathos.

> *"Thirdly, persuasion is effected through the speech itself when we have proved a truth or an apparent truth by means of the persuasive arguments suitable to the case in question."*[21]

The appeal to logic and reason is the most broadly understood form of persuasiveness for a legal argument. Legal readers expect it and respond immediately to practical and logical arguments. To effectively use logos, you want to use the logic of the argument itself to persuade, and make sure that your argument indeed follows a logical, stepwise progression. You will persuade the court to decide the case favorably for your client by showing how the law and its application *require* a ruling in your client's favor, and that it is not subject to another correct interpretation. But logic alone is not usually persuasive in close legal questions. Along with maintaining a high standard for your professional reputation, your ethos, you need also to appeal to the pathos of your client's situation.

Storytelling Your Theme

Pathos is most effectively created through storytelling. Stories are fundamental to how people learn, process, and understand the world around them. Experiments in cognitive psychology show that when information is presented in a familiar context—as part of a story structure—it is much easier to remember than if presented in a less familiar way.[22] In the legal realm, storytelling is at the heart of what lawyers do. "Every legal case starts with a story—the client's story—and it ends with a legal decision that, in effect, offers another version of that story ..."[23] Stories are important in legal work because they can help make the reader or listener understand a complex legal issue more easily—when it is placed in a framework that we have all used before and are intimately familiar with.

---

20. *Id.*

21. *Id.*

22. *See, e.g.*, Richard O. Lempert, *Why do Jury Research?, in* Inside the Juror (Reid Hastie ed. 1993).

23. J. Christopher Rideout, *Storytelling, Narrative Rationality, and Legal Persuasion*, 14 J. Legal Writing 53, 53 (2008).

Of course, humans have been telling stories, listening to stories, and understanding stories from a young age, which makes them a kind of universal language for all of us, including judges. But stories need to have "narrative rationality,"[24] that is, they have to make sense to the reader or listener. The story that is consistent, plausible, and complete is more likely to be accepted by your listener. In contrast, a story that leaves out key details, or glosses over the importance of certain details a reader would find important, will strike that reader as false or unreliable. The importance of narrative rationality is particularly strong in legal storytelling because lawyers work in the realm of competing stories—the stories they construct in their advocacy for clients are subject to being tested against the opposing counsel's story on behalf of his or her client.

In legal writing, the best place to detail your client's story is found in the statement of the facts and in your theory of the case. Wherever you are explaining the background and facts of the case you have an opportunity to tell your client's story. Look for opportunities to make your client sympathetic, and to set what happened to your client in a narrative that sounds like a story we are familiar with. Has your client been wronged by the faceless corporation? Has she been the subject of harassment in the workplace? Is he a small business owner being put out of business by a burdensome regulatory scheme? The goal is to tell such a coherent and compelling story that it leads the reader to want to agree with your theory of the case.

Literary Devices

The use of imagery, vivid language, and other literary devices in your writing can make it more persuasive. If you can tell a compelling story that also paints a vivid picture in the mind of your reader—so, for example, they can *see* and *feel* the sting of the workplace harassment—it can also help to convince your reader that your theory of the case is the correct one. Two common literary devices are alliteration and repetition. A powerful example of these persuasive techniques can be found in Dr. Martin Luther King, Jr.'s *Letter from Birmingham Jail.* In his letter, written while imprisoned in Birmingham, Alabama, during the civil rights marches, Dr. King uses alliteration and repetition to make his readers understand why African Americans can no longer wait for desegregation but must take non-violent action.

> "Perhaps it is easy for those who have never felt the stinging dark of segregation to say, "Wait."
>
> *But when you* have seen vicious mobs lynch your mothers and fathers at will and drown your sisters and brothers at whim;
>
> *when you* have seen hate-filled policemen curse, kick and even kill your black brothers and sisters;
>
> *when you* see the vast majority of your twenty million Negro brothers smothering in an airtight cage of poverty in the midst of an affluent society; ...

---

24. *Id.*

when you have to concoct an answer for a five-year-old son who is asking: "Daddy, why do white people treat colored people so mean?" ...

when you are harried by day and haunted by night by the fact that you are a Negro, living constantly at tiptoe stance, never quite knowing what to expect next ... *then you* will understand why we find it difficult to wait."

In this passage Dr. King uses a series of vivid examples set off by the repetition of "*when you*" in an effort to persuade his reader that the time for waiting has passed. Images evoked by such language as "smothering in an airtight cage of poverty" and "hate-filled policemen [who] curse, kick and even kill your black brothers and sisters" evoke visceral reactions in most readers. The persuasive power of the letter is accomplished not only by its subject but by the brilliant use of imagery, vivid language, and alliteration as found in the repetitive "k" sound words *curse*, *kick*, and *kill*.

While most legal documents will not deal with injustices as heinous as those fought by Dr. King, each piece of legal writing designed to persuade presents the opportunity for the writer to go beyond the basics of the IRAC form and to use a broad range of writing skills to persuade the court of the justness of the client's position. Whenever you are acting as an advocate for your client, look for opportunities to tell the client's story and to do so coherently and with power.

Further Reading

Antonin Scalia & Bryan A. Garner, *Making Your Case: The Art of Persuading Judges* (West, 2008).

Ruth Anne Robbins, Steve Johansen & Ken Chestek, *Your Client's Story: Persuasive Legal Writing* (Wolters Kluwer, 2012).

Exercise

Write a two-page memo addressing Dr. King's *Letter from Birmingham Jail* following the instructions from your professor.

As You Prepare This Assignment, Consider the Following

What about Dr. King's letter was persuasive?

What did you find unpersuasive, and why?

How might the persuasive techniques Dr. King used in his letter be applied to a legal document?

Reflect about the sort of impact the letter had on you, and what that means to you as you prepare to become a lawyer. What kind of professional do you want to be in the law?

ONLINE: Martin Luther King's Letter from Birmingham Jail.

Chapter 12

Legal Letters

Introduction

Lawyers write legal research memos, and they write documents that are submitted to courts, such as legal briefs. But more often they write letters, and increasingly in today's world they write email messages of all types. The kinds of correspondence that lawyers write can vary considerably, often depending on their practice area. Of course, like any business person lawyers write transmittal letters—"Enclosed with this letter is a copy of ..."—which are increasingly now sent in the form of email messages: "Attached to this email message is a draft of...." While these can be important, they do not usually contain a great deal of legal analysis. But lawyers do write letters that contain significant legal analysis and sometimes advocacy on behalf of their clients. Among those are opinion letters, demand letters, and settlement letters, each of which has a different purpose.

The Opinion Letter

An opinion letter is written to provide a client with a legal opinion on a question of law as applied to certain facts. An example is a letter written by a lawyer offering an opinion as to whether a certain provision of the tax code applies to a set of financial facts presented by his or her corporate client. Similar letters are written by lawyers addressing questions of the applicability of certain auditing requirements, sufficiency of title in a real estate transaction, or applicability of state or federal regulatory requirements to a client's business or planned transaction.

An opinion letter offered to a client will follow a predicable (and by now familiar) form. After an introduction, a statement of the issue is offered along with a summary of the opinion being given. This is followed by a statement of the facts that has been given to the attorney—this part is important because you want to be sure the opinion is based expressly on the set of facts that you were provided by the client. This is followed by an explanation of the applicable law, and an application of that law to the facts provided by the client. Then the legal opinion is reiterated, and that is followed by a closing, which usually recommends next steps that the client might want to take, given the opinion and guidance you provided. Usually a legal opinion will also have specific warnings and limitations, such as that the opinion is limited to the facts recited, only useful for a limited period of time, or only applicable in certain state jurisdictions.

Some opinion letters are a required part of a transaction that involves a business loan. For example, banks normally require that a borrowing corporation's lawyer issue a legal opinion in support of the credit agreement offered by the bank noting that the corporation is duly licensed, authorized to do business in the relevant state(s), is in compliance with all securities laws, and is in good standing. Lacking such an opinion letter, the bank will not make the loan. These types of legal letters follow a fairly strict form, and sometimes the provisions to be included are specifically required by the bank. If you become a transactional lawyer, you will want to follow a senior attorney's methods and forms for drafting such letters, since they have significant legal consequences.

A variant of an opinion letter is an advice letter. This sort of letter is written to the client, often as a summary of a counseling session that has already taken place between the attorney and the client. It provides a summary of the meeting, reviews the applicable law, and offers options for the client to consider before the attorney proceeds in her representation of the client. When reviewing the applicable law that was discussed, you should remember that your audience for an advice letter is typically not a lawyer so you will need to explain complex legal principles in simple terms, and you will generally not need to cite to case law.

Remember that it is always the client's decision how to proceed with the matter and not yours. An advice letter often uses the legal research that a junior attorney has prepared, and may even include a copy of the legal research memorandum written by the junior attorney. The letter and the memo are designed to provide advice about the client's legal options. This is distinct from an opinion letter, which offers a concrete legal opinion on which the client can, and likely will, rely.

The Demand Letter

A demand letter is written by a lawyer on behalf of a client who has hired him or her to help resolve a dispute. It is usually written before litigation or other action commences. The letter may be written directly to the person or entity believed to be the cause of the dispute but will almost certainly be shown to an attorney soon after its receipt. A demand letter notifies the party about to be sued, as well as that party's attorney, that litigation is pending, and it offers that party an opportunity to avoid litigation. It describes the facts that lead up to the dispute, the nature of the claim being made, the legal principles upon which it is based, and the damages that were incurred by the party making the claim. Finally, it usually offers terms for an early resolution of the matter. These generally include the full amount of the claimed damages although also included might be a request to repair something damaged, or to complete an unfinished project. When you draft a demand letter you should, of course, provide a copy to your client.

A demand letter seeks to persuade the opposing party that they should accept your proposed terms and resolve the matter prior to litigation. Because it is a persuasive document, you should take the discussion of persuasion in the previous chapter into account when drafting such a letter. And since it is written to an attorney, or will likely be reviewed by one, you should include the statutory and case law upon which the claim is based. There is no reason to reveal weaknesses in your analysis as you would in an internal legal research memo about the matter. Keep in mind also that ethical considerations attach to a demand letter. In all their dealings lawyers may not make "a false statement of material fact or law to a third person."[25] This prohibition applies to anything a lawyer might say or write. Thus you will want to be careful as you describe the facts that lead up to the dispute in your demand letter, and as you describe the law that you argue should be applied. Keep in mind that in most cases a demand letter is threatening enough on its own and is thus not in any way improved by histrionics or inflated claims.

Finally, you will want to put a time limit on the demand you are making and be clear about what will happen after the time limit expires. You may not hear anything in response to the demand letter you send on behalf of your client. Should you receive no response and the matter remain unsettled you need to have a date when you know your offer has been constructively rejected.

The Settlement Letter

A settlement letter is written by a lawyer on behalf of a client who is already embroiled in a dispute. Sometimes such a letter is written early in the dispute; sometimes it is written later on after the ensuing lawsuit has been active for some time. Like a demand letter, a settlement letter is a persuasive document, and it usually includes terms of an offer based upon which your client is willing to settle the pending dispute. Like a demand letter, it includes a recitation of the facts and a persuasive argument based on the applicable law. But unlike a demand letter, the terms offered to settle the matter are usually not for the full amount of alleged damages but rather some reduction of the amount based upon factors determined in the litigation so far.

When offers of settlement are made in a dispute, the terms of the proposed settlement are not admissible at trial under Federal Rule of Evidence 408.[26] This rule is designed to encourage settlement discussions, and to deter attempts for one party to use at trial an admission or willingness to settle as an inference of culpability. Just as with a demand letter, in a settlement letter you need to include a time limit after which the settlement offer expires. That way you have a date certain after which the settlement offer is withdrawn, and you can proceed with the litigation knowing that it was effectively refused.

Professional Email

Most of what you have already learned about legal writing also applies to legal writing in the form of an email. This is for some a difficult adjustment to make, since

25. Model Rule of Prof'l Conduct R. 4.1 (1983).

26. State Rules of Evidence in virtually every state have a similar rule.

many of us are used to using email mostly for informal communications. But you want to be professional in your email correspondence, and pay just as much attention to editing and proofreading as you would with any other legal document. Abbreviations, lack of capital letters, and emoticons are not appropriate in professional email correspondence.

Before you send your client an email, consider whether a written letter would be more appropriate for the purpose of the communication. An opinion or advice letter is still usually printed and sent via regular mail. Consider also the confidential nature of the correspondence with your client and be circumspect with sensitive information or data. It is still common for demand and settlement offers to be in the form of letters, even if these letters are sometimes attached to an email transmission and not also sent via regular mail.

It is particularly easy to make mistakes with email correspondence. Be aware that mistakenly sending confidential correspondence to opposing counsel is a violation of the ethical rule of confidentiality.[27] While the standard disclaimer and request that the information be returned unopened might make you feel better, it should not. It is still a violation of the ethical rules to transmit client information to an opposing party. Be particularly careful with the "Reply All" feature of email software since often this is where attorneys make this mistake.

Email allows us to communicate more quickly, and we are used to the speed that it provides. But, as with all legal work and professional correspondence you should slow down and take your time so as to avoid careless errors. This is particularly true of email.

Further Reading

Steven D. Stark, *Writing to Win* (Three Rivers, 1999).

27. Model Rule of Prof'l Conduct R. 1.6 (1983).

Exercise

Draft a demand or settlement letter (whichever your professor assigns) to opposing counsel in the problem presented in your final memorandum from the fall semester. Also, respond to the email assignments that are sent to you by your professor during the course of the semester.

As You Prepare This Assignment, Consider the Following

Who is the audience for your letter?

Does your letter accurately describe the facts of the dispute?

Does your letter explain the legal principles upon which your demand or offer is based?

Have you been clear about what terms you are demanding or offering?

Have you clarified the time limit on your demand or offer and what will happen if you do not receive a response?

ONLINE: Examples of client advice, opinion, and demand letters.

Chapter 13

Legal Briefs

Introduction

Legal briefs are persuasive documents filed in court in connection with a pending case. In a brief, the lawyer's role is that of an advocate; the brief is the primary device through which a lawyer persuades the court to agree with his or her client's position. Throughout the brief you want to strive to present the law in a manner that establishes the validity of the client's view of how the law should be applied to the facts.

A legal brief differs from objective legal writing in three main ways. First, a brief must be persuasive as opposed to a fully objective statement of the law (such as in an internal office legal memo). Second, the brief should present the law in a way that, if accepted by the court, will lead to a positive outcome for the client. Third, a brief should tell a story—the client's story—in a compelling way.

Ethics

A lawyer has at least two roles, that of an advocate and that of an officer of the court.[28] One's duties as advocate are eclipsed by the duty of candor to or honesty with the court. Thus a brief should argue for the interpretation of law favorable to the client, but should not go so far in the argument as to misstate the law or hide relevant adverse facts in a cited case. Similarly, the story that you tell in the facts section should include all facts, both favorable and unfavorable. Otherwise you risk the court coming to the conclusion that you cannot be trusted, which would obviously undermine your reputation and credibility with the court.

Types of Arguments

In briefs, there are primarily four types of legal arguments that are used: arguments from precedent, interpretive arguments, normative arguments, and institutional arguments. Most effective briefs use combinations of these types of arguments to give the deciding court the best reasons, on a variety of grounds, why it should decide in favor of your client.

28. *See id.* R. 1.3, R. 3.1, and R. 3.3 (and accompanying comments).

Arguments from precedent are the standard legal method for applying law to the specific facts in your case. When you construct a legal argument based on precedent, you are arguing that the precedent must be followed because the facts are meaningfully similar to your client's case. Or, you may be arguing that the precedent should be extended to an analogous situation. Or, you may be arguing that the precedent case should not be followed because the facts in that case are meaningfully different or not sufficiently analagous to the present case. Finally, you may be arguing between two conflicting lines of precedents. Such an argument looks like this: Line A of conflicting legal precedents should be followed because.... These are the most common forms of legal arguments based on precedent. A persuasive legal brief might use a mixture of these forms of argument.

An interpretive argument is based on the plain meaning and legislative history of a statute. Here you are arguing that the plain meaning of the statute should be applied and that the plain meaning is X. Or, alternatively, you might argue that the statute is ambiguous and the court should interpret the statue in this way because Y. You might also argue that the plain meaning of the statute conflicts with the legislative history and the legislature intended for the statute to mean Z. These are all forms of interpretive arguments.

Normative arguments are based on accepted standards of public policy (what is good for society as a whole) and justice (what is just and right). For example: "innocent victims must be compensated," or "a ship owner should ensure that those operating his vessel are competent," or "plaintiff should not be rewarded for 'sleeping on her rights.'" Normative arguments can also be arguments based on economics and a cost-benefit analysis. For example, "limitations on maritime liability will promote maritime commerce."

Finally, institutional arguments address the appropriateness of the case before the court. For example, you might argue that this decision is one that courts are best equipped to make, or alternatively that this decision is one belonging to the legislature. An institutional argument might also take the form of an argument that if the court were to decide the case as your opponent suggests, it would "open the floodgates" to future litigation that would hinder the judicial process.

Choosing Your Issues

Often there are many different issues upon which you can make a legitimate motion or appeal, and you want to pick the winnable issues. Although that seems obvious it involves more analysis than you might think. Selecting winnable issues of course involves deciding which issues, based on precedent and other factors, have the greatest chance of prevailing with the particular court. Choosing which are most likely to prevail is based on the quality and depth of your research into the court, its judges, and case precedent, and researching the standard of review. For example, if a lawyer does not conduct thorough research, he may not discover that the court in which his client's case is pending has decided a string of cases favorable to prisoner's rights; depending on your client's situation, the court's stance on prisoner's rights may be good or bad. Furthermore, knowing the court's prior holdings may convince the lawyer to frame his arguments to include a prisoner's rights argument or, alternatively, base the argument on the Eight Amendment to the Constitution.[29]

When arguing a case before an Appellate Court, understanding the applicable standard of review is important in deciding which issues to argue because each standard of review carries a different level of deference to the lower court. Those issues that have "*de novo*" standard of review call for no deference to the lower court and are the most attractive to appeal because the reviewing court is not bound by any prior decisions in the case. The "*arbitrary and capricious*" standard of review is the next best, because it calls for only moderate deference to the lower court. As you research the applicable standard of review, you should use it to help prioritize the arguments you will make in your brief. If you have the option, you should generally avoid issues that require the court to review errors that are "*clearly erroneous*" because this standard of review provides the most deference to the lower courts.

Sections in the Brief

Introduction: Title Page, Table of Contents, Table of Authorities

The title page of a brief is the caption for the case where the parties and case number are listed. The title page should follow the specifics outlined in the court rules (or those outlined by your professor). The Table of Contents and the Table of Authorities come next, and are there for the convenience of your reader. The table of contents lists the pages on which each section of the brief begins. The table of authorities should list *all* of the authorities you cite in your brief (cases, statutes, articles, legislative history, etc.) and each page on which the authority is cited (including *id.* citations).

One of the reasons briefs include a table of authorities is to allow the reader to compare your brief and your opponent's brief side-by-side. For example, a judge may be particularly interested in how the lawyers on both sides address a particular case. The table of authorities would list the case and all the pages on which it appears, so that the judge can easily find each lawyer's analysis of that case. In contrast, if the case is not listed in the table of authorities, the judge can immediately identify that the lawyer may have missed an important part of the issue before the court. Judges use the table of contents and table of authorities in briefs in myriad ways, and that— and also because they are required by court rule—is why we include them.

Statement of the Issues

The statement of the issues section is where you present the summary version of your arguments for each of the issues in your brief. Even though a summary, you want to already be telling your client's story and presenting your theory of the case

---

29. The Eighth Amendment to the U.S. Constitution protects prisoners from being subjected to cruel and unusual punishment.

in this section. A formula you can use to generate a first draft of each of your statements of the issues is:

> Whether [facts/circumstances] constitutes [legal standard] under/within the meaning of [legal statute or rule], when [X, Y, and Z facts are present].

Here is an example statement of the issue in a brief:

> Whether delay caused by an inmate's transfer to a new prison constitutes "justifiable excuse" within the meaning of § 16-5-402, when the inmate was not transferred until two weeks before his notice of appeal was due, the prison mail system was functioning properly, and the inmate had access to the prison library.

When you have more than one issue in your brief, the question immediately arises: which should come first? Generally, in a brief you want to emphasize your strongest points first, so organize your issue statements with that in mind. Of course, the argument section of the brief should be organized in the same order as you have them in your statement of the issues.

Statement of Facts

Just as with a statement of facts in a legal research memo, in a brief's SOF you should only include the key determinative facts to the case. Therefore, if it is not crucial to the case that the accident happened on December 13, 2012, do not include the date in your statement of facts. However, if you are arguing a statute of limitations issue where the date matters, be very clear about all the dates involved.

Unlike in an interoffice legal research memo, where you will evenly include all relevant facts, in a brief you should emphasize your best facts and deemphasize any unfavorable facts. You might even leave out facts that are favorable to the other side but are not necessary to a fair understanding of what happened in the case. But be careful before doing that. If there is a key fact and much of the case turns on that fact, you might damage your ethos to the court if you leave it out. Where you need to include it, deemphasize its importance through the use of passive voice, or directly addressing its value to understanding the case.

The question of how best to refer to the parties in a brief is a reasonable one, but there is no widely accepted approach, other than the advice to strive for clarity. In a trial court, it is helpful to your reader to refer to the parties as either Plaintiff or Defendant, because that reminds the judge of the relationship between the parties in the lawsuit. But often it can be even more helpful to refer to the parties by the roles that they held before the lawsuit, such as "Landlord" and "Tenant," or "Lessor" and "Lessee," since that provides more information to the reader. In an appellate court, referring to the parties as "Appellee" and "Appellant" is often used, but this again only provides information about which party sought the appeal; it does not indicate which party was the plaintiff in the lower court, and it also does not indicate anything about the relationship between the parties before the lawsuit was filed. In trial briefs, some attorneys will refer to their own client by their first name, and the opposing client by "Mr." or "Ms." or by the party's title, in an attempt to personalize their client by comparison. There are few rules about these options; clarity is the higher goal.

Statement of the Case

The statement of the case section in a brief describes how the case has proceeded through the lower courts and the reasons why the case is appropriately before the current court. For example, you might write in this section:

> At trial in Denver District Court, the defendant was found guilty of robbery in the first degree. Upon defendant's appeal to the Colorado Court of Appeals, the appellate court reversed, finding that the defendant was not provided effective assistance of counsel because counsel was denied to him during the pleading phase. The state now appeals the appellate court's decision and seeks reversal of the appellate court and reinstatement of the defendant's conviction.

Depending on the complexity of the applicable standard of review, you may want to include the standard of review for the issues in the brief under a separate heading or within the statement of the case. A simple standard could be included at the end of the statement of the case. Where you have multiple standards of review, or if there is a dispute about the appropriate one to apply, the explanation of the standard(s) of review should be included in a separate section. The standard of review should be a concise statement describing the standard for the first issue, followed by an appropriate citation. For example:

> Because the question before the court is one of statutory interpretation, the appellate standard of review is *de novo*. United States v. Moore, 567 F.3d 187, 190 (6th Cir. 2009).

Summary of the Argument

The summary of the argument section is just what it sounds like—a summary of your argument. Think of it as a "10,000 foot" view of your brief as a whole, but somewhat more forcefully stated than the conclusion. This section should include a more detailed explanation of the law as well as a more detailed application of the law to the facts of the client's case. The summary of the argument section of your brief provides an additional opportunity to tell your client's story and to emphasize your theory of the case.

The Argument

The argument section of your brief includes several elements and—like the discussion section of a memo—is the heart of the document. An argument section in a brief begins with point headings. Point headings are a persuasive statement of your conclusions that appear right after the section heading. The point headings should orient your reader to your arguments and provide signposts for changes in topics. Be careful not to make them too long—you should be able to read your point heading out loud in one breath. For example:

I. JIM'S LIST IS A PLACE OF PUBLIC ACCOMMODATION BECAUSE IT FITS WITHIN THE ADA'S REQUIREMENTS AND HAS A NEXUS TO A PHYSICAL PLACE

The sub-sections of your brief begin with sub-headings, which are also affirmatively stated, and which briefly summarize what follows them. For example:

A. *According to the Plain Language of the ADA, Jim's List Qualifies as a Place of Public Accommodation.*

B. *The ADA Applies to Jim's List because there is a Sufficient Nexus between the Website and Its Physical Place of Business.*

Under Section I above, and before the sub-sections, there should be an overview paragraph for each issue that includes a brief rule explanation and application of that rule to the facts. In the overview paragraph, the rule and rule application should be stated generally. This is much like the overview paragraph you would write for a multi-issue legal research memo.

Next, using the above example, there should be a thesis paragraph under sections i, ii, and B above. This thesis paragraph should include a more specific rule explanation and rule application than in the overview paragraph. In each of the rule statements and explanations the rules should generally be statements of law synthesized from other cases. Remember that a synthesized rule is not a list of cases. When you synthesize a rule of law, you are gathering the legal principles from several precedent cases and condensing them into one statement. For example:

> When a court considers whether the defendant had a reasonable fear of imminent death or great bodily harm, it considers three factors: (1) the deceased's possession of a weapon, (2) the physical differences between the deceased and the defendant, and (3) the defendant's history of violence.

Lastly, after the rule statements and explanations, the brief should apply the stated rule to the client's facts. In this section, the lawyer analogizes or distinguishes the precedent cases addressed in the rule explanation section and offers a conclusion about how the court should apply the law to the client.

Responding to Opposing Arguments

For the most part, you want your brief to be focused just on your client's arguments. Giving "air time" to your opponent's arguments by addressing them individually in your brief is generally unnecessary and can be counter-productive. However, occasionally, even without reading your opponent's brief you may know that they will rely on a particular case, or make a particular argument. If that argument is a concern to you, it may make you decide to address it in your own brief, to preempt the strength of the argument, and perhaps to undermine it somewhat.

Be aware that in most jurisdictions it is an ethical violation to not cite a case that is directly opposite to the position you are advocating to the court. There is some room for interpretation as to what is "directly opposite" but to avoid damaging your credibility with the court, you should include and address the opposing case if there is any doubt.

If your concern is about a particular case, you have four primary options for addressing the concern. First, you can distinguish the case based on differences between the facts of that case and the facts of your case. Second, you can distinguish it by making an argument that the reasoning of the court does not apply to your client's facts. Third, you might explain how the rationale behind the reasoning of the court is incorrect by checking the authorities used by the court to see if they were wrongly applied or decided. Fourth, you may explain how the principle in the case is no longer sound public policy.

Conclusion

The conclusion section of your brief should be a short restatement of what you are asking the court to do and one sentence relating to each issue regarding why the court should decide the case according to your request. For example:

> The district court's order denying defendant's motion to dismiss should be affirmed because Mr. Canato properly stated a claim for relief in his complaint. The plain language of the ADA and supporting case law indicates that Jim's List is a place of public accommodation and that Jim's List has a nexus with its headquarters. Congressional intent further supports the classification of Jim's List as a public accommodation and the ADA's purpose of eliminating discrimination against the disabled requires that the ADA apply to physical and virtual locations.

Finally, you need to include your Prayer for Relief, which is simply a statement of what you are asking the court to do. For example: For the foregoing reasons, Appellee requests that this court affirm the district court's denial of Appellant's motion to dismiss.

Further Reading

Ross Guberman, *Point Made: How to Write Like the Nation's Top Advocates* (Oxford, 2011).

Bryan A. Garner, *The Winning Brief: 100 Tips for Persuasive Briefing in Trial and Appellate Courts* (2d ed., Oxford, 2004).

Exercise

Draft a trial and/or appellate brief for the legal matter provided to you by your professor.

As You Prepare This Assignment, Consider the Following

Do your point headings pass the "one breath" test?

Does your statement of facts contain only the necessary facts to the case?

Have your persuasively told your client's story?

Did you include a procedural history and standard of review?

What is the standard of review that governs your issues? How does this influence whether you should use this issue?

Have you provided an overview to your argument section?

Does your argument section use the correct format, including point headings, overview paragraphs, thesis paragraphs, rule statements and explanations, and an application to the client's facts?

What types of legal arguments have you used and how are these types of argument effective?

What issues can you bring before the court? Which of these issues are the strongest?

ONLINE: Example Trial Brief and Example Appellate Brief.

Chapter 14

Oral Argument

Introduction

As a practicing lawyer, no matter what your area of practice, you will have numerous opportunities to advocate your client's positions orally, in the spoken word. One way to learn this skill is through learning how to prepare and present an oral argument to a court. Even if you do not end up working in an area of law that involves court appearances and making such arguments, these skills will be transferable to other oral presentations you will need to make as a lawyer.

An oral argument before a court is a conversation between the lawyer and the bench. When a court requests an oral argument (or grants a request from an attorney) the court is seeking an opportunity to engage you more deeply and directly about your arguments than they can by only reading your brief. Oral argument is not the time to debate with the court, but instead is an ideal time to inform the court of your client's position and an opportunity to explain why that position is the most logical and just outcome.

There are three purposes to an oral argument. First, oral argument should enhance the lawyer's motion or appellate brief without rehashing each argument in the brief. Second, during oral argument you should make an effort to rebut your opposing counsel's arguments. Third, and most important, during oral argument you must answer the court's questions. This chapter provides an overview of the differences between trial and appellate court oral arguments, offers methods for preparing for oral arguments, and suggests ways to predict and prepare for questions from the bench.

Trial Court—Motions Arguments

In trial court, attorneys will present oral arguments at a motions hearing. Motions hearings cover topics from admissibility of evidence, to discovery disputes, all the way to dismissal of an attorney from a case based on a conflict of interest. Almost always, oral arguments at trial are presented without a jury being present. However, the timing for oral arguments varies. In some cases, lawyers may have requested a specific sort of motions hearing prior to trial, for example, a *Daubert*[30] hearing where admissibility of expert testimony would be ruled upon. In most other instances mo-

30. *Daubert v. Merrell Dow Pharm.*, 43 F.3d 1311 (9th Cir. 1995).

tions and their arguments are heard immediately before or just weeks or days before trial, and serve to narrow or limit the issues that will be addressed at trial.

Generally, oral arguments in trial court are faster paced and shorter than oral arguments in an appellate court. This is because a trial judge will often hear arguments on several different legal questions at once. The time for oral argument for each question therefore is brief. Also, keep in mind that trial courts are *busy* and motions are not their primary function; the primary function of a trial court is hear evidence, find facts, and deliver a verdict. In a trial argument, the party who filed the motion will begin oral arguments with an argument for its position and offer a proposed action for the court. The party defending the motion will then state its reasons for opposing or objecting to the "moving" party's position and propose an alternate action for the court (such as denying the motion). The judge may interrupt either side's presentation at any time with questions.

During an oral argument before a trial court, a lawyer will address a mixture of questions of law and questions of fact. Questions of law deal with statutory interpretation, case law, and the jurisdiction of the court. Questions of fact deal with the facts of the case currently before the court and analogies between those facts and case law. Admissibility of evidence is often very fact-specific and trial judges are interested in a direct comparison of the facts in the present case and facts in the case law. When it comes to questions of law, trial courts most often adhere to precedent and are reluctant to "make new law" or expand prior precedent to an analogous situation. This is because their function is not to interpret the law, but instead to apply the current law to the current facts of the case. Therefore, in the trial court questions of law are usually limited to what the applicable statute indicates and how that statute has been previously interpreted. Trial courts do not generally welcome public policy or "expansion of the law" arguments.

Appellate Court Arguments

Appellate court oral arguments are more structured and more formal than trial court arguments. Before hearing an oral argument, the judges assigned to hear the arguments will have read all the briefs on both sides and have conducted their own case law research. Lawyers who appear before the appellate court in oral argument should assume that the judges have reviewed the briefs submitted by both sides to the court.

As in trial court oral arguments, the party who filed the appeal goes first, followed by the party defending the appeal. At the appellate level, the party making the appeal also has a chance for rebuttal following the defending party's presentation. The appealing party must have reserved time for rebuttal at the beginning of his presentation. Thus, the order for an appellate argument goes like this:

Appealing party (Appellant)

Defending party (Appellee)

Rebuttal—(Appellant), if time was reserved

Each side will usually have 30 minutes in total for its case-in-chief. For appellants, the 30 minutes includes the time reserved for rebuttal.

The substance of your argument will resemble a truncated version of the brief you prepared. In the introduction part of the argument, you introduce yourself to the court and introduce your co-counsel (if you have one), and introduce your client (if he or she is in attendance). Then you briefly introduce the issues in the case. The most important part of the introduction is the request for relief. This is when you make a specific request as to what you would like the court to do. For example: "We request the court affirm the lower court's finding that the Jim's List website is a place of public accommodation under the ADA." The introduction of the case should only take a minute or so.

After the introduction, you offer the court your theme for the case and give the court a roadmap for the argument you will present. The roadmap is derived from your point headings for the two or three most important arguments that you made in your brief. After offering a roadmap to the court, you should continue to use these "signposts" when switching topics; these signposts should match the topics mentioned in the roadmap paragraph.

In the argument section your goal is to engage in a conversation with the court. Remember "oral argument" is a misnomer—lawyers presenting before an appellate court are not *arguing* with anyone; the focus is on the judges, not on opposing counsel. Oral argument is the time to present the two or three main points of your case and address the court's concerns. The argument portion of your oral presentation should boil down the argument section of the brief to two or three main points, with a focus on rule applications. The main points you offer to the court should be the strongest arguments for the client, the topics that are most likely to concern the court, or a combination of both. You will not have time to address every argument in your brief. Pick the two or three that are most important and stick with those.

An oral argument should end with a conclusion that reflects back to your roadmap paragraph. The last thing you want to say before you sit down is to reiterate the request for relief—express again (and finally) what it is your client wants the court to do. If you run out of time during your conclusion, stop speaking immediately, and ask the court for extra time to conclude. If the court grants some extra time, finish your point briefly, state your request for relief, and then sit down.

If you represent the appellant, reserving time for rebuttal is a good argument strategy. Rebuttal comes after the appellant's case-in-chief and after the appellee's presentation and is reserved during the appellant's introductory remarks. Because only one to three minutes are typically reserved for rebuttal, do not save any of your main points for that time. Instead, rebuttal should focus on responding to the appellee's arguments. In forming a rebuttal, the appellant should pay particular attention to the appellee's argument and the court's questions to the appellee to identify the points that most need a response. Because of the short time for rebuttal, lawyers for the appellant should make only one or two quick points and then sit down. Rebuttal is typically not prepared in advance; you will prepare your rebuttal while listening to the appellee's case.

Questions During Oral Arguments

The reason that oral arguments are considered a conversation rather than an adversarial argument is because of the questions you will get from the bench. At any time during the presentation of oral arguments, the bench, usually consisting of three or more judges, may ask the presenting attorney questions. While oral arguments in trial court are typically limited to narrow questions of law and fact, appellate court oral arguments can include a broad range of questions. These questions can be about applicable law, facts, parties, public policy implications, or economic arguments.

When one of the judges asks a question you should stop speaking immediately even if you are in the middle of a sentence. Before answering you should make sure you have heard the entire question. The best way to make sure you have heard the entire question and have understood it is to take some time and pause before answering. The pause gives you time to think about your answer and make sure you understand the thrust of the question and what the judge may be seeking in asking it. The answer itself should be direct. This means if the question calls for a yes or no answer, you should first say "Yes (or no), your honor" and then explain your answer. After you have finished your explanation, you should transition back to the argument you were making before the question was asked. Some tips to help you develop the skill of making transitions easier and smoother are included in the preparation section below.

The lawyer who is fully prepared for oral argument welcomes questions from the bench because it gives him or her the opportunity to converse with the court about questions or problems the court has with his or her case and request for relief. Thus, you should anticipate and welcome questions, but do not assume that the bench will be vocal and keep questions coming the entire presentation period. Some benches are "hot" and barely let you finish your answer before asking another question, while some are "cold" and ask few questions. You need to prepare for both types.

There are several types of questions that judges may ask during oral argument. Among these are questions that go to background, scope, and implications of your argument. Background questions are about the parties, the opinion or the record below, or about how different courts have ruled on the same issue. Scope questions are about the position of the party the lawyer represents, details about the cases that may be dispositive of the issue, statutory text, legislative history, or policies underlying the rules put forth in case law. Questions concerning scope may also come in the form of questions seeking concessions in your argument, for example, "Counselor, do you concede that the defendant was fleeing from the police before he was apprehended?" Concession questions are particularly useful to the court but can be very dangerous for the unprepared lawyer. (If the fact of fleeing is central to the court's decisions in prior cases, conceding that fact may significantly harm the lawyer's argument). Finally, implications questions are those that may ask about the "slippery slope" that may result if the court grants the client's request for relief. These types of questions also include hypotheticals, questions about analogous legal contexts, and questions about whether the court is the correct institution to decide the issue (as opposed to the legislature).

While the court is most likely to ask questions that go to background, scope, or legal implications, you should also be prepared for questions that are somewhat random and thus hard to predict. Judges were lawyers once, and sometimes they will ask questions that come out of their prior professional experience or their personal knowledge. These kinds of questions are hard to prepare for in advance, but if you are well prepared overall and you know your case well, you will be able to handle these occasional questions just as well as the more typical questions that judges ask in oral argument.

Preparation for Oral Arguments

Oral arguments are action-packed and go by quickly. The key to a successful and relatively low-stress oral argument is preparation, preparation, and more preparation. By the time oral argument comes around, you should know both the law and your opponent's cited cases inside and out. You should also have memorized your introduction, and have created a map or diagram of your argument to facilitate answering questions and making easy transitions between issues.

The first step in your preparation includes solidifying your knowledge regarding the procedural background of the case, the relevant facts of your case (and where to find those facts in the record), and the relevant law. Being knowledgeable about the relevant law includes knowing the source of that law, i.e., statute numbers and sections and case names (although you will not usually be required to provide a full citation to a case, since those are in your brief). It is usually a good idea to have a paper list or index cards with key facts and citations to the record so that if the court asks, you can easily direct their attention to the relevant support for further review after oral argument.

As part of your preparation for oral argument, you want to focus on and refine your theory of the case and the theme of your argument. Every oral argument should have a theme; the theme will connect the story of the case with the arguments for the relief that you seek. A theme can be as simple as, "The ADA should not be interpreted to include websites as places of public accommodation because the added costs will destroy small businesses." Or, in the alternative, "The ADA includes websites as places of public accommodation because to conclude otherwise would be contrary to the intent of the ADA to bring the disabled into the mainstream of the American economy." The theme could also be several sentences that include both a policy theme and a theme based on precedent.

After developing a theme, you will want to create an outline of your oral argument that includes just the two or three major points that you consider most important or that you believe are most likely to win the case for your client. Your outline should also include notes about rebuttals of arguments that may be made by the other side. Remember, when lawyers prepare for oral argument, they have the brief(s) submitted to the court by opposing counsel and therefore have a good idea of the other side's arguments.

Preparing your outline is only the first step in your preparation, and it should not exceed two or three pages. While you are presenting your case to the bench you do not want to be flipping through pages trying to locate notes on the next point you want to make. If you can, you might want to take the time to extend the outline to a longer script. The script should be one or two minutes under the allotted time for argument. Once you have that you can practice it. Practice your script in front of the mirror, in front of friends, or in front of your pet. But, do not try to memorize the script (other than the introduction) because memorization may lead to inflexibility in moving to other topics when prompted by a question from the bench.

You probably do not want to take your script into the courtroom for the same reason that you should not take an outline—it is just too many pages. Your script will be several pages long so the best thing to do after practicing your script repeatedly is to reduce it to a one page "map" or other visual representation of your argument. This map will keep you organized in your argument, and help you locate and transition to a point after being asked a question. Remember, judges do not have to follow your roadmap in asking their questions. If you have announced a roadmap that will deal with points A, B, and C, the court may well ask questions on points B, C, and then A. Having a map of your argument will help you with transitions even in this situation because it will allow you to see, on one page, all of your argument points and the connections between them. Some lawyers even color code their maps so that each issue has a color to facilitate transitions by just a glance at the map (and some practice with it).

Even if you have prepared and practiced thoroughly, it is possible (although rare) that you will be asked a question by a judge that you do not know the answer to. There is, unfortunately, no good way to address such questions. Pretending you do know the answer is not a good approach, so it is better to own up to it, offer to file a supplemental brief with the court addressing the question, and then transition back to your argument.

Now that you have your preparation completed, on argument day what should you bring to the podium during oral argument? First, it is best not to bring a pen or other object that you might be prone to fiddle with while at the podium (i.e., no pocket change and no excess paper to shuffle). A good way to organize materials for oral argument is in one manila file folder. When you open the folder, on one side might be the oral argument map and on the other might be a reference guide for cases, statutes, and citations to the record. Staple your map and reference sheet to the folder so that the pages do not move or fall out (or fall to the floor). It is also a good idea to have memorized your introduction and roadmap paragraph. Knowing the first part of your oral presentation by heart will help put you at ease and reduce the normal feeling of nervousness. Once you have given the introduction you will find your presentation rhythm and will be able to address whatever questions the judges decide to ask.

Further Reading

David C. Frederick, *The Art of Oral Advocacy* (2d ed., West, 2010).

Bryan A. Garner, *The Winning Oral Argument: Enduring Principles With Supporting Comments from the Literature* (2d ed., West, 2009).

Exercise

Prepare an oral argument for your appellate problem. Practice it with your co-counsel, and practice it again with your professor or teaching assistants (if possible). Then give your final oral argument following the instructions of your professor.

As You Prepare This Assignment, Consider the Following

In your introduction, have you included a request for relief?

What arguments do you want to discuss with the court? Why have you chosen these arguments?

Have you included the arguments you would like to address in your roadmap?

What questions do you anticipate?

What do you think opposing counsel will address in their argument?

Have you drafted transitions to help return to your argument after addressing a question?

Have you practiced in front of others? What questions did they have about your argument? Did you know how to answer these questions?

What are you planning to bring with you to the podium? How are you going to map your argument and transitions?

Have you memorized your introduction and roadmap paragraph?

ONLINE: Examples of an introduction, outline, script, map, and reference sheet for oral argument.